For all the wonderful children and families
in the Down syndrome community
who have taught me so much
and inspire me every day.

Table of Contents

Acknowledgments

Many people supported me through this process and taught me a great deal along the way. Thank you to my wonderful team at Boston Children's Hospital; to Dr. Emily Davidson for her incredibly helpful commentary and edits; to Susan Stokes, editor extraordinaire; to Woodbine House for giving me this opportunity; to my wife for her endless patience and support; and to all the children and families with whom I have the pleasure of working.

Introduction

Behavior challenges in individuals with Down syndrome (DS) are incredibly common. In fact, about 30 percent of children with DS have behavior issues that are significant enough to be diagnosed by a psychologist (such as myself) or another health care professional. For a bit of context, typically developing children are diagnosed with behavioral disorders only about 10 percent of the time (McCarthy, 2002). Even more children with DS have more minor behavior problems. These behaviors may not require a professional's help, but they can still cause problems at home and at school. This book will help you, as a parent, teacher, or any other adult who interacts with individuals with DS, understand the cause of these behaviors and how to manage them effectively.

Challenging behavior is so common among people with Down syndrome that it no longer surprises me when I travel to speak about behavior in DS and find rooms overflowing with people eager for some help. So, the first thing I hope you realize when reading this book is that you are by no means alone.

Second, I want you to know that when left untreated, behavior problems in children with DS tend to persist. In other words, children with DS who have behavior problems oftentimes become adults with DS who have behavior problems. And if an individual with DS has behavior problems in adulthood, that can limit where that person can live, work, and socialize very significantly. After all, would you want to live or work with someone who might hit you or destroy your stuff? So, when I am working with children and families, I see behavior problems as a really big deal, and something that can make or break how things go later in life for a person with Down syndrome. The goal for the individual with DS is to have the most fulfilling adult life possible. Behavior can really get in the way, so we have to deal with it effectively when it becomes a problem.

The third point that I always have in mind when I am working with behavior problems in children with DS is that, with the right interventions, *things usually do get better.* In other words, it may take some time and effort, but I very rarely find that problem behaviors are "unfixable." This is particularly true for the majority of people with DS, who are often quite sociable and eager to interact with and please others. Because most people with DS *want* to be successful behaviorally and make other people happy (what a wonderful trait!), this gives us a big head start when we are tackling challenging behaviors.

The first step to understanding behavior problems in individuals with DS, in my opinion, is to understand how the brain works for this wonderful group of people. Children and adults with DS have so many wonderful attributes, which is why the late Dr. Allen Crocker, the founder of our Down Syndrome Program at Boston Children's Hospital and Harvard Medical School, used to wear a pin on his lapel that stated simply, "Up Syndrome!" However, some of these very same brain differences, such as being very sociable and emotionally attuned, can actually have big and sometimes negative behavior implications if not understood and addressed. The goals of this book are to help you, as a reader, understand how the brain works in people with DS, how the world around us may be a mismatch for this particular brain profile, how the mismatch can lead to behavior problems, and most importantly, how to help people with DS do their best behaviorally.

As you read through this book, please keep in mind what I consider my guiding light for all of my work with children and families—your relationship with your child, student, or patient with DS. Decades of research have demonstrated that for all mammals, from tiny ones such as mice, all the way up to human beings, the parent-child relationship, also known as attachment, is an incredibly powerful and important part of life. This relationship helps us to learn to regulate our bodies and our minds, and it benefits both children and parents. I believe that this connection can be expanded to include teachers, clinicians, and therapists as well. Thus, as you read through this book and as you experience difficult behaviors, keep in mind that your relationship with your child, student, or patient is the most important factor. And when you don't know what to do, consider what is best for your relationship and move in that direction.

I hope that this book will be helpful to parents, teachers, and clinicians who are caring for or working with children and adolescents with DS from about age two until young adulthood. While this book does cover a wide range of people with DS, some of the ideas are general and may not be a good fit for each individual. I also cannot begin to describe *every* behavior problem or intervention out there. While there are some very good behavior books that cover a far wider array of problems and interventions, I have found that when we suggest a 300-page book to busy parents, they often do not have time to read it. As a result, I intentionally tried to keep this book focused and not too lengthy. The book is also based on the concept that the broader ideas are the most important things for you to understand. If you can understand the major concepts, you are most likely going to be able to understand and manage behavior much more effectively and to think creatively about how to do so. In fact, I usually tell people when we start working together that my goal is to be fired. No, I'm not a huge fan of *The Apprentice*. Rather, I want families to understand these concepts so well that they can apply them themselves, without my help.

The concepts presented in this guide can be applied creatively to a range of issues. Still, you might need more support and input from professionals. So, I encourage you to read through this book and learn about how the brain works in Down syndrome and what behavior tools are likely to be effective. At the end of the book, you will find resources you can seek out if and when further help is needed.

About the Author

In case you are wondering about my qualifications to advise you on behavioral challenges in Down syndrome, here is a brief background. I started spending time with people with DS in my early childhood. My mother, a now-retired special education teacher, had a best friend who was in charge of the developmental disabilities program in our local community center. As a child and teenager, I spent many weekends at fundraisers and activities for, and with, people with disabilities. Many of the participants had Down syndrome. I remember these events fondly and came to have a deep affection for this group of people. It also did not hurt that I am a huge basketball fan, and many members of the Boston Celtics were often in attendance at these events. As I progressed through my own development, I was always counseled (or in other words, required) by my family to be open to the wide range of differences among people. This is deeply engrained in me.

I feel very much at home in this community, as I have throughout my lifetime. Further, the children, adolescents, and young adults with whom I work, and their families, are incredibly positive, resilient, and often just really nice people to be around. I love my work and come home feeling that I have learned and gained more from the children and families I see than they have from me. As Yogi Berra is reported to have said, "I haven't worked a day in my life." So, while I do this for a living, I do so with a deep appreciation and respect for the individuals with whom I work, and from whom I learn so much.

And now for a brief blurb about my professional training and background. I often begin lectures by telling people about my first job after college, as a "child behavior specialist." I had a degree in clinical psychology with a focus on child development, and I felt I knew what I was doing. However, when I was actually put on the job, I was pretty terrible at managing children's behavior. My basic guiding principle was "I'm the adult and what I say goes!" Anyone who is reading this book probably can imagine how terribly that went.... Still, this experience got me excited to learn more about how I could do better.

After college, I pursued my doctorate in clinical psychology, and during my training I gained experience working with children, adolescents, and adults who were doing quite well at a college counseling center, and adults in a locked inpatient unit who were in more serious states of mental illness. I was able to learn about the history of our understanding of the mind, from Freud and psychoanalysis, to Pavlov and Skinner—the forefathers of behavior theory. During my doctoral training, I had exposure to a wide variety of issues and people. However, I continued to feel most comfortable working with those with developmental challenges. I found my professional home at Boston Children's Hospital and Harvard Medical School, where I completed my fellowship in pediatric psychology, focusing on neuropsychological testing and behavior therapy.

When my boss approached me in the second year of my postdoctoral fellowship and asked if I would be interested in working in the Down Syndrome Program, I jumped at the chance. I immediately felt at home, and began conducting testing and behavior therapy with a group of children, adolescents, and families that felt incredibly familiar to me. Over the past several years, I have worked with hundreds of children and families with DS. I have seen improvement, and often really amazing improvement, in many if not most cases. I have been lucky enough to speak all around the United States, in Canada, and in Europe about behavior and DS, and have found that these very simple ideas, combined with a solid understanding of DS, really do work.

It has been my honor and privilege to engage in this as my "job," and I was equally honored when I was invited to share what I have learned in this book. Thank you for taking the time to read it. I hope it will help you, the reader, to help those with DS be successful behaviorally and developmentally, and to lead the happiest and most productive lives possible.

Chapter 1

How **Not** to View Behavior in Individuals with Down Syndrome

Parents, teachers, or other adults often view negative behavior from any child as willful or intentional. In other words, it certainly feels to us adults that a child who is misbehaving *wants* to upset us. Indeed, even in my own experience as a pediatric psychologist, it certainly *feels personal* when a child hits me or destroys the toys I have given him or her. However, as a behaviorally trained clinician, I firmly believe that all behavior has a purpose. It is a form of communication. No child or adolescent wakes up in the morning thinking, "How can I make my parents or teachers miserable today?" Rather, behavior is a means of expression when we have no other tools left in our skill set.

An analogy that I often find useful for parents is to think about going to work. Imagine that every day you walk into work, your boss tells you

what to do all day long, every second. Now imagine that your boss also keeps telling you that you are doing your job all wrong and constantly corrects you, even though you are trying your hardest. How long would it take before you wanted to leave that job? And what if you couldn't leave, like a frustrated child in a school program that is not a good fit? How long would it be before you acted out in some way? What other choice would you have aside from misbehaving?

Consider these examples:

William is six years old. He has Down syndrome and some behavior problems. As he sits in my office and his parents speak with me about these challenges, William plays with some toys for about fifteen minutes. Then, as his parents and I continue to talk, William grows bored. He runs over to the light switch and turns it off. All of a sudden, and very quickly, all the adults in the room are paying a lot of attention to him, raising our voices and scrambling to get the lights on. His parents look to me and say, "See what we are dealing with!?"

My response to situations such as these often surprises families. That is, I usually respond by saying that I am not doing a very good job of structuring William's environment and his time in my office. I gave him some toys to play with, but the toys are not all that interesting to him. So, when he "acts out" by turning out the lights, is it really that William is trying to upset us adults? Or is it his way of communicating, as he does not have very much language, that he needs something else to do and would like some attention?

*Jennifer is a thirteen-year-old girl who is in the seventh grade. She loves to read, even though it is hard for her at times. She cooperates during reading class, but when it ends, she starts to act out. In fact, when her teacher says, "Okay, it's time to head to math class in the next room," Jennifer drops to the floor and hides under a desk. She refuses to move, makes silly noises, and even kicks the adults who come near her to try to move her along. Her teachers are at their wit's end since this happens every day. Again, it certainly **feels** to her teachers as if Jennifer is just being difficult and wants to make them miserable. And since the teachers are viewing this behavior as willful, they naturally react by punishing Jennifer. They give her time-outs, take away her iPad, and write notes to her parents about her bad behavior.*

But what if we think about this behavior differently? If Jennifer is only hiding under a desk when she is asked to go to math class, maybe there is a problem with math. I would want to know how she is doing in math and what type of instruction she is receiving. Perhaps we need to adapt the curriculum, or she needs to do math individually or in a small group rather than in a larger classroom. Again, the behavior is not meant to drive the adults crazy. The behavior is Jennifer's way of telling us that she is not getting what she needs. It is a form of communication.

As you can see, the impact of **how we view these behaviors** is tremendous. If we view them as willful, or intentional, we immediately begin to think about how to *punish* William and Jennifer. And this punishment would be very ineffective, most likely. But if we consider these behaviors to be a communication that William needs something more interesting to do and that Jennifer is having trouble in math, we would respond to William's behavior by providing him with more toys and to Jennifer's behavior by changing her math instruction. By taking this second approach, we would actually be meeting each child's needs. And they would receive support, the behaviors would improve, and everyone would be happier. If we punished William, his behavior is unlikely to improve (more on this later), and we would all be upset. The same is true for Jennifer.

Nobody likes to be punished, and adults generally don't like to be the ones punishing, either. So remember, depending on how we understand and view behaviors—as a willful act designed to annoy the adults, or a form of communication of a need or a problem—our response is vastly different.

As the examples above illustrate, a helpful place to start is to acknowledge that the child's or teenager's behavior is not a willful act that is designed to make you upset. Rather, it is an expression of some unmet need or challenge that is not being addressed. When you can take this perspective, you are way ahead of the game. You can respond to behavior thoughtfully, rather than emotionally. You can learn to respond...*but don't react*. And, as we will see throughout this book, emotional responses to behavior problems in people with DS can be really destructive.

The next basic idea that I find very helpful is that **behavior management is often not intuitive.** Rather, some of our instinctive reactions, such as yelling or being rigid and sticking to a "rule," can really backfire for those with DS. It's almost as if we have to turn off some of our gut reactions to behavior problems in order to have a chance at managing them more effectively. So, getting upset, talking about behaviors extensively, yelling, using the old-fashioned time-out, grounding, and holding firm to rules may need to go out the window for now. After all, if we think of Jennifer and her refusal to go to math class, we can imagine how being rigid would backfire. If we say, "Jennifer, it's time for math—you have to go," she is not likely to respond well. After all, we are not addressing the true problem. Rather than following our "orders," Jennifer is likely to act out even more.

But not to worry, in the following chapters, I will provide you with plenty of other options and some clarifications about how we can modify these tried-and-true behavior management tools to be more effective for those with DS.

Chapter 2

Why Do Individuals with Down Syndrome Have Behavior Problems?

This is an exciting time to work in any health care field that deals with problems "above the neck." Neuroscience has made great strides in understanding how the brain works, including in people with Down syndrome (DS). Some wonderful neuroscientists such as Drs. Lynn Nadel, Deborah Fidler, and Jamie Edgin have made great contributions to this field that have led to a far better understanding of how the brain works in people with DS. Using this understanding of strengths and weaknesses, we have a giant head start in knowing how to manage behavior in DS.

It is important to note, however, that as in any group of people, there are many individual differences among children, teens, and young adults with DS. So, some of the brain differences that are discussed here may not apply to every person with DS. Indeed, we often conduct extensive neuropsychological testing to figure out how an individual child's brain works. Still, we do know about some general trends in DS, and these trends provide us with big clues as to why behavior challenges occur in individuals with DS, and more importantly, how best to manage them.

• •

Learning and Memory

The first big difference in the brain for individuals with DS lies in the area of learning and memory. Two key areas of the brain, the *hippocampus* and *temporal lobe*—which are both very important for learning and retaining new information—are quite different in DS. When a typically developing child learns something new—either by hearing it explained or seeing it in action—her brain processes that information and then "encodes" it by transferring it to longer-term memory. Next, her brain "consolidates" the information, or stores it permanently. The most crucial difference for children with DS is that new information is not transferred into long-term memory and stored as easily or as consistently.

This difficulty transferring information to long-term memory probably accounts for the common observation that children with DS often learn best with repetition and review of concepts or tasks, rather than being expected to learn something that is explained only once. Seeing or hearing about a topic only one time may not allow a child with DS to hang on to the information.

I often think of the learning process for an individual with DS as being quite anxiety provoking. Imagine if information was being presented to you at a very rapid pace, all day, every day, and your parents or peers seemed to comprehend it easily, but you did not (not yet, anyway). Or think about how you feel when you travel to another country where the people speak a different language that you do not understand. It is very tiring and frustrating to try to keep up! It wouldn't take very long before you became really, really frustrated.

This difficulty with learning and remembering new information is just one of many reasons that I believe individuals with DS benefit so much from routines. Routines make the world a more predictable place. It is soothing for all of us to know what's coming next. Think about it: if you are in a foreign country where you may not understand what's happening around you, knowing what's coming next will be infinitely more valuable and anxiety-reducing for you than being constantly surprised by your environment.

Visual vs. Verbal Learning

This brings us to our next brain difference, which is that individuals with DS tend to be far stronger visual than verbal learners. For those with DS, the parts of the brain that process visual information are often stronger and better developed than the portions that process language. (This is a very oversimplified way of viewing this, of course.) You might notice, for example, that for many children with DS, saying the same direction over and over such as "Go to the potty" is ineffective. But when you produce a picture of the potty, your direction seems to come alive.

This relative strength in visual processing has become even more apparent with the evolution of technology. I have see countless children with DS who struggle with language but can navigate an iPad far better than I. This pattern of strengths and weaknesses also plays out in neuropsychological testing. When professionals test children with DS, we typically see stronger scores on nonverbal/visual tasks than on language-based tasks.

If we put together the first two brain differences in DS, we know that 1) routine is crucial to help with information processing and keep anxiety at bay and 2) it is easier for children with DS to understand information that is presented visually than verbally. Remember these pieces of information for later, when we turn back to a discussion of drawing on typical visual strengths of individuals with DS to help them establish and follow routines.

• • • • • • • • • • •

Language

Given what I mentioned above about language weaknesses, it may seem that language is hard for individuals with DS, period. However, it's not so simple. In fact, language development is very complex, and children with DS usually have a particular profile of relative strengths and weaknesses.

For most children with DS, *receptive language,* or the ability to understand what others say, is stronger than expressive language, or the ability to express their own thoughts, wants, or needs. This can be very frustrating for a child. For example, imagine if you could understand everything around you, but you accidentally put crazy glue on your napkin at lunch and glued your mouth shut. As a result, you had no way of telling people around you what you thought or what you needed. Now imagine that this was not a single occurrence but happened every day of your life. How frustrated would you be that you could understand so much but had no opportunity to tell people what you thought or what you needed? How long would it be before you resorted to other means, such as aggressively taking what you needed or hitting people because you had no way to tell them they had upset you? Again, it can be very frustrating to be able to understand so much without being able to tell others what *you think* and how *you feel* to the same degree.

An interesting phenomenon also occurs for a smaller group of people with DS who have the opposite profile. I have seen several children and adolescents who have developed strong expressive language skills and can speak clearly, in full sentences, with a great vocabulary. For many of these individuals, however, their receptive language, or understanding, does not match their expressive language. This can cause others to overestimate their knowledge and to hold them accountable for things that they may not necessarily understand (for example, making comments about sex or repeating lyrics from violent movies or songs).

I have worked with some adolescents with DS who have picked up a great deal of vocabulary related to relationships and sexuality. Often, these teens are referred to me by very concerned school staff who worry that these students are being abused or having sexual experiences. Of course, that possibility needs to be investigated and ruled out. However, on several occasions I have found after a thorough evaluation that these children simply have far stronger expressive vocabulary skills compared to their receptive ability to understand what they, or others, are saying. So, even though they easily learn new words and can repeat them quite clearly, they may not understand what they are saying. Rather, they have said some of these words and seen strong reactions from peers, teachers, and parents. This has led to them to conclude that these are "fun" words, despite not fully understanding their meanings. Or, they may understand the meanings very well but not use the best judgment about when and how to use those words. Naturally, this can cause big problems for children and families.

● ●

Executive Function

The next brain difference that we see in individuals with DS relates primarily to the frontal lobe, and that is the area of *executive function (EF)*. EF is, in basic terms, a set of processes in the brain that allow us to do the things we want to do, or to meet our goals. These executive functions enable us to plan, organize, be aware of our progress, sequence our steps, remember what we have done and what needs to be done, and control our impulses if we become distracted or see an easier but incorrect way to finish the task. EF can also determine the speed at which an individual processes or understands information. The child with weaknesses in executive function may need more time to understand a teacher's question and to formulate a response, for example.

For adults, good EF skills may enable them to finish a task at work by a certain due date. For children, EF skills are crucially important for many aspects of daily life. For example, if a child is instructed to finish a worksheet before recess, she must sit down and focus, plan out her approach, work in sequence, remember the instructions, and control those impulses to just run outside!

At home, EF is also important in enabling children to plan out and prioritize how they spend their time. For example, if a child with good EF is told she cannot play with the iPad until her brother is done and she has finished her homework, she may choose to sit and finish a math worksheet, knowing her turn will come. But if a child with EF difficulties knows that she can play with the iPad after her brother is done, she may struggle to resist her impulses and grab the iPad from him in the middle of his turn, even though this will get her in trouble and lead to less time playing with her favorite toy. If you ask her after the fact, she can probably tell you this was the wrong decision, but her impulses and trouble with planning out her behavior got the best of her. This behavior is very similar to what we see in people with attention-deficit/hyperactivity disorder, or ADHD. Russell Barkley, PhD, author of *Taking Charge of ADHD,* often says that ADHD (which is generally speaking a disorder of executive function) is "not a disorder of not knowing what to do. It is a disorder of *not doing what you know*" (emphasis added).

Each of the executive functions—planning, organizing, keeping track of your progress and the quality of your work, and resisting impulses—is typically somewhat weaker for people with DS. The good news is that the frontal lobes, where executive functions live for the most part, continue to develop into young adulthood, and I have seen many of my patients with DS improve dramatically in their EF. In fact, many parents are relieved when I tell them that those "little kid impulsive behaviors," such as bolting and hitting, will probably get better on their own over time. But still, we often have to build in some external executive function supports, especially for younger children. For example, children may need to be given reminders to stay on task, have work broken into smaller steps to help them plan and organize their approach, and be given reminders to control those impulses.

A good example of a behavior that results from challenges with executive function is bolting, or running off from adults. I have worked with many children with DS who have a hard time "staying put," despite being very willing and eager to please their parents and teachers. For example, I worked with a little girl who ran off when her parents weren't looking and when her teachers left the classroom door open. This behavior culminated during a charity walk, when the child ran away from our entire group in a very large open public area. Naturally, I was horrified to witness this. And the kicker was that I was the one who was supposed to be "fixing" the problem! This little girl was very engaging and cooperative generally. However, when she saw something she was interested in, she went for it. She did not "stop and think" or consider the consequences of her behavior. She did not *plan* her actions. On this occasion, after a very scary thirty minutes, we found her playing a basketball game about fifty feet away, happy as a clam.

Over time, we developed lots of external supports to help her remember the rules. This helped build in some external executive functions to help her stay out of trouble. And over time, as she developed, many of these behaviors improved and we did not need to work so hard to keep her safe. You will read many similar examples of behavioral improvement throughout this book.

Social Functioning

People with Down syndrome are often thought of as incredibly social. Particularly in the past, when individual differences were perhaps less of a focus, people with DS were described as *universally* sweet, fun to be around, and loving. Indeed, this is often the case, as the brain profile in DS often does lead individuals to be very sociable. Parents, siblings, teachers, and service providers often find interacting with children and teens with DS to be very rewarding, and I have certainly experienced this many times.

Heather Nyapas Photography, on behalf of the Down Syndrome Association of Pittsburgh

It is important to acknowledge, however, that there are also many people with DS who struggle with social skills to a certain degree. Some may be shy and yet very sociable with close friends and family, but less friendly or responsive to others, particularly new people. Individuals with DS who are shy may avoid group activities in school or family gatherings, preferring to play alone in their bedrooms. For another subgroup of people with DS, even basic social skills such as making eye contact, smiling back at someone, and playing an interactive game such as peekaboo may be very challenging. If these difficulties are accompanied by communication problems and unusual behaviors such as repetitive movements or fixations on particular toys or topics, we sometimes need to consider another diagnosis such as autism spectrum disorder (ASD).

To make things even more complicated, many children with DS are very interested in others and love to interact with and gain attention from other people. However, some studies have shown that people with DS have reduced "social problem-solving" skills. In other words, the individual wants to interact but may not know how. As a result, we may see a young girl with DS who hits all of her peers in preschool, or an older boy with DS who sits alone at lunchtime and avoids interacting with classmates. Often, these very same children with DS would like to interact more positively with their peers but simply do not know how to do it.

Interestingly, if a person with DS is very social and outgoing, this can also cause or exacerbate some behavioral challenges. On a brain-based level, social reactions from other people are very powerful. I like to refer to this as the "Social-Emotional Radar," and it is often very strong in those with DS. As we have discussed, language skills in children with DS are not usually so powerful. As a result, when negative behaviors do occur and an adult says words that are clearly meant to *discourage* the behavior (such as "Don't do that or you'll be in big trouble!"), the child with DS often does not process the actual words. Instead, she *only* processes the social response. So, the effect is as if the adult's words are said in the voice of the nanny from the *Muppet Babies,* or the parents in the Charlie Brown movies, "Mweh mweh mweh." In other words, the child hears the sound, but the words are meaningless.

And at the same time, the message being received in the child's brain is like winning a slot machine. The child thinks, "It's very exciting to see my dad looking right at me, with a very strong facial expression, making lots of noise! This is fun!" The words and their meaning are not being processed, but the emotion certainly is. The result is that the social response of the adult becoming animated and giving lots of attention, positive or negative, far outweighs whatever the adult is saying.

Another aspect of social functioning in DS that can be problematic is that, as a result of being so connected to others on a neurological level, people with DS are also exquisitely sensitive to losses. My colleague Dr. Kerim Munir, together with my group from Boston Children's Hospital and I, have written about this in various publications. We have found that for people with DS, separation from peers, a teacher, or one-to-one aide; the death of a loved one; a sibling going to college; or even the transfer of a peer to a different classroom can hit a lot harder than we might expect. So, when we see children with DS who are experiencing behavioral or emotional challenges, we often ask about losses to see if this might be playing a role.

Still, despite all the challenges that the social profile of those with DS can pose, socialization is a crucial element of brain functioning that we can use to manage behavior effectively. I often tell parents and teachers that *your most powerful tool is you.* The facial expressions, tone of voice, and nonverbal cues that you offer to a child can be more powerful than any other reward or any punishment. For many children with DS, praise and attention from a parent, sibling, or teacher is far more powerful than any other reward. And taking away attention and emotional responses is a far worse punishment than a time-out or losing a toy, which is surprising for most people. We will return to this later.

· · · · · · · · · · · · ·

Motivation

The final key brain difference that we will focus on for this book is in the area of motivation. Intrinsic motivation and task mastery are sorts of "inner drives" that make us want to finish tasks and do them well, even in the absence of external rewards such as praise or money. Some research suggests that individuals with DS have a decreased inner drive to complete tasks. For example, if a ten-year-old boy who is typically developing is struggling with learning his times tables, he may sit and work at it for hours, or even days and weeks, to finally get it. In contrast, a ten-year-old boy with DS may try to work on a new math concept for a while but become frustrated or silly and then try to distract his teacher with a bright smile and talk about his favorite movie. He may do anything he can to avoid those math problems the next day. Of course, not all children and teens with DS use such avoidance tactics, but some do.

You may be asking, why does this happen? Well, if we take a step back and consider all the challenges with language, executive functioning, learning, and memory described above, it is pretty easy to see that many tasks are more challenging for individuals with Down syndrome. Just as a child who has an injured leg uses more energy to walk down the street, so does a child with DS use more energy than his typically developing peers to complete classwork, process his teacher's spoken language, sit at the dinner table and talk to his family, and brush his teeth before bed.

As I have a soft spot for cars, I often use car analogies for the brain. And I like to call this the *Gas in the Tank Theory.* Quite simply—we all start the day with a certain amount of gas in the tank. If you have a disability, each task takes just a little bit more gas. Over time, that gas is depleted more and more, and you become fatigued and frustrated. This may occur more quickly in people with DS than with children or adults who do not have some of the same brain differences. In my observation, I have seen this cumulative "gas in the tank" phenomenon countless times, and I believe that it plays a major role in motivation differences in people with DS.

Now that we have reviewed many of the brain differences in DS, let's take another step back and think about the world in which we live. It includes a great deal of language, work, social interactions, and emotions. I like to think of our world as a "perfect storm" of demands that directly challenge multiple areas of weakness for individuals with Down syndrome. For me, then, it is no surprise that behavior problems are so common in people with DS.

Chapter 3

Behavior 101: Learning Theory

Understanding how people learn, including how they learn behavior (behavior theory), can be complicated. But the basic principles are really very basic, thanks to the psychologist B. F. Skinner. What Skinner discovered—which now seems obvious to us because it is built into our culture and language—is that we need to "reinforce" behaviors that we want to see more of, and not reinforce the bad behaviors. In other words, we provide "good stuff" for behaviors we want others to repeat (e.g., good behavior), and we *do not* provide "good stuff" for behaviors that we want to go away (e.g., bad behavior). It's that simple, in theory. But in reality, applying these simple principles becomes pretty difficult when you add in all the complexity of human interactions, language, emotions, and brain differences.

Proactive or Reactive? Helping Children with DS Behave at Their Best

When considering how to manage behavior, many families, teachers, and providers think first about discipline. In other words, they ask themselves, "How can I make this behavior stop?" Remember, this is particularly likely to be your reaction to a behavior if you do not understand its cause. If you think the behavior is occurring simply to make you crazy, you will likely try to end it with discipline.

Naturally, negative behaviors can be frustrating, and we all want to stop them as quickly as possible. However, once a behavior has occurred, we are already behind. We are reacting to the behavior rather than preventing it. Similar to looking after our heart health, we would much rather *prevent* the problem by eating well and exercising than have to *react* to it after becoming sick. In addition, when we react to a behavior rather than prevent it, we are usually emotional. We are only human, after all. For example, when a child destroys one of my neuropsychological tests or the few remaining toys that still light up and make music in my office, I can't help feeling frustrated. But I know that my frustration is not going to help the situation. So, even if I feel perturbed, I have to ensure that my reaction is based on a better understanding of the behavior instead of letting my emotions get the best of me.

Interestingly, while most of us think about discipline when we see problem behaviors, research has consistently shown that proactive strategies simply work better. Proactive strategies are just like they sound. They are techniques that we adults can put into place to help *prevent* negative behaviors and promote positive behaviors. Examples include setting up a rewards system or using a visual schedule. We will talk about plenty of these in the pages to come. Proactive behavior strategies are so effective, in fact, that the federal special education laws specify that "positive behavior supports," or proactive strategies, must be tried first for managing problem behaviors, rather than reactive strategies such as punishment. Positive behavior supports/proactive strategies are what this book primarily focuses on.

Reactive strategies, or what we do after a behavior has occurred, include some effective tools such as discipline, removal of privileges, and time-out. However, discipline can often be a slippery slope and can devolve into ineffective methods such as yelling, shaming, or even spanking. These methods have been shown to be less effective over the long term and some (e.g., spanking) can have harmful effects as well.

Consistency and the "Slot Machine" Theory of Behavior

Behavior management can be a tricky business. There are many positive behavior support methods that are simple to use, prevent negative behaviors, and promote positive behaviors. And there are strategies, such as ignoring, that are very effective in reducing negative behaviors once they occur. But even though these strategies are very easy to understand, they can be hard to maintain over the long term. I often tell families, teachers, and providers that I can explain behavior in just a few seconds: reinforce the good stuff; don't reinforce the bad stuff. However, keeping this up over many months and years is far more challenging.

A crucial part of maintaining effective behavior management is consistency. For example, let's say that Christopher is jumping on his sister's bed and loving the reaction he gets from his sister, who yells, laughs, and sometimes cries in response. In this case, ignoring Christopher's behavior might be very effective, for it is likely the attention that is keeping the behavior going. However, if Christopher's sister ignores the behavior effectively, but then his little brother comes into the room and laughs hysterically, all of a sudden jumping on the bed has become really fun again and is likely to continue. Christopher has been reinforced on an inconsistent basis. That is, sometimes he is reinforced by a sibling laughing, and sometimes not. Inconsistent reinforcement actually makes the behavior even worse—Christopher is likely to keep jumping on the bed even longer, because he has learned that he may get a reaction if he does the behavior long enough.

To use reinforcement effectively, not only family members but also different caregivers and providers must respond to a behavior consistently. For example, perhaps a child's teachers are effectively ignoring a particular behavior. But if the parents are not aware of this plan, they may react with very emotional facial expressions and loud voices saying, "Stop that right now!" This inconsistency is going to make the behavior recur.

Let's consider Aliya, who has been making "poop" noises or "raspberries" whenever she is asked to do some schoolwork or homework. At home, her family has learned to ignore the behavior and pretend it is not happening at all. And sure enough, Aliya has been making raspberries less and less. But when she has a substitute teacher at school for a week, this new teacher finds the noise intolerable and "inappropriate." She raises her voice to Aliya and gives her a time-out. All of a sudden, that behavior has become pretty interesting and gets Aliya lots of attention. And sure enough, when she comes home, she is right back to square one, making raspberries all evening until she falls asleep.

Responding inconsistently to behavior is a very powerful way to make behaviors continue. If you are looking for an example of this principle, you need look no further than any slot machine. Slot machines are designed based on "variable ratio reinforcement schedules." In other words, the rate at which you will win is constantly changing and totally unpredictable. As a result, people are drawn to keep putting money into the machine because "maybe this will be the time" that they will win. When we do not respond consistently to a child's behavior, either between people or over time, we are creating the same type of "schedule" and likely making that behavior even worse. The child is likely to keep trying the behavior out because *maybe* this will be the time he gets a reaction!

This is why Christopher persists in jumping on his sister's bed. Even though his sister is ignoring the behavior, he thinks that if he keeps doing it, *maybe this will be the time* that his little brother comes in and gives him a big reaction!

The Nuts and Bolts of Behavior Management: Helpful Terms & Concepts

So, let's make this a little more complicated and break down what reinforcement really means. In essence, reinforcement means that we are doing something that increasements the likelihood that someone will engage in a given behavior. For example, if a child is beginning to talk or use the potty on his own, we might want to *add* something, such as praise or excitement, to make that happen more often. Some other behaviors we may wish to reinforce may be things a child is already doing or that only happen once in a while. These may include activities like the following:

- getting dressed independently,
- putting away toys,
- clearing the table,
- hanging up a towel after a bath or shower,
- feeding the family pet.

Positive Reinforcement

Most often when we talk about reinforcement of children with DS, we are talking about using positive reinforcement. That is, we *add* something as a reward, of sorts, when we want a behavior to continue to occur or to occur more frequently. This "adding" of something to reward a behavior is where the word *positive* comes in, and we end up with the term *positive reinforcement*.

Often the response I hear from families when I recommend using positive reinforcement is something along the lines of this: "So we have to bribe our child for good behavior?"

Really, reinforcement is in no way a bribe. It is providing an environmental reward and incentive for doing good things. It is similar to the paycheck that adults receive. When a parent or caregiver goes to work and receives a paycheck, is that a bribe? Or is he or she just being rewarded by the environment for the work that he or she did? This is an important distinction that you have to understand before you can really get started with positive reinforcement.

The next issue that families often face is deciding how to reward their children. Many families feel so motivated that they want to commit to giving their child a big reward—by buying a toy every day, taking a trip for ice cream every night after dinner, or making some other big commitment of time or money. But choosing reinforcement does not have to be so hard. If we think back to how the minds of children with DS work, we know that they are generally

very sociable. So, on a neurological level, a big reward often comes not from prizes like toys or ice cream, but from *other people*. In other words, you do not usually need to give your child a concrete reward—buying a toy or taking him out for ice cream—to reinforce a behavior. Instead, you can think of yourself, your facial expressions, your emotional reactions, your eye contact, and your *attention* as the most powerful rewards and reinforcers of all.

We will come back to this later, but, for now, let's remember that positive reinforcement is, quite simply, adding something that a child likes to increase the odds that he will repeat a behavior. And the reward that you add does not have to be something expensive or inconvenient; it is actually more likely to be effective if it comes in the form of attention and recognition from you.

Since the attention of a parent or other adult can be such a powerful reward, we need to be very conscious that sometimes attention that we don't intend to be reinforcing can become reinforcing. This is where positive reinforcement becomes quite tricky when parenting and working with individuals with DS. Since we know that the language center is not as strong as the social center of the brain, much of what we say may not be understood, or at least not in the way we would hope. This is particularly true if we are emotional when we are speaking.

Think about a child running into the street. This is a very common behavior among children with Down syndrome. Understandably, parents become very upset and animated as they chase their child, which they have to do. In these situations, parents typically run after the child while making lots of eye contact, screaming, and yelling. I would do the same!

However, if we think about the brains of children with DS, we know that the child may not be processing all the words such as "Watch out," "Be safe,"

"Get back here right now!" Rather, what the child is processing on a very basic brain-based level is that Mom, Dad, or the teacher is very, very animated and he is getting lots and lots of attention! He is receiving a lot of neurological "reward" for this behavior, as he gets to watch people become very worked up, screaming and yelling, with lots of emotion. The words are likely being drowned out by all the emotion and attention, if they were even understood at all. Believe it or not, in this situation, we are actually *positively reinforcing the behavior.* By yelling, making eye contact, and becoming very emotional, we are *adding* something that is very rewarding for the child with Down syndrome. This makes the child more likely to repeat the behavior.

We will discuss how to manage our own emotional reactions to negative behaviors later, but let's keep in mind that when we do become emotional and animated, we are likely reinforcing whatever behavior is happening. So, while our emotions can be difficult to manage, we need to remember that our own reactions are also our most powerful tool.

Negative Reinforcement

Now, a few other important terms related to behavior. I often hear people talk about "negative reinforcement." People often think that yelling or becoming upset is a form of negative reinforcement. It does make some sense; yelling and becoming upset sure sound negative. And they surely can make behaviors happen over and over. But this is not what behavior specialists mean by *negative reinforcement.* Let's break it down and focus on the actual terms. *Negative* means to take something away. *Reinforce* means to encourage a behavior to recur. So, negative reinforcement means to take something away to make a behavior occur again and again. As usual, an example is most helpful.

Let's think about William, who starts to yell and throw his books and papers on the floor when math starts. When he does this, his teacher takes him out of the classroom and to the principal's office. The next day, guess what? William throws his stuff on the floor when math starts. Why? Well, despite the best intentions, the teacher removed the unpleasant thing (e.g., math), making her response "negative" in behavioral terms. Since she removed something that William dislikes, this reinforced the behavior of throwing items on the ground. William got to escape math class, the thing he does not like, by throwing his stuff on the floor. So, the behavior was "negatively reinforced."

Negative reinforcement is a concept that is good to know about and to keep in mind, particularly when a new behavior pops up that you cannot figure out. When you are facing a behavior that does not seem to make sense, it may be that the behavior is being reinforced inadvertently by someone *removing* something that the child does not like. It is not such a useful tool for behavior management, but it is something to be on the lookout for when behavior is challenging.

Punishment

The next very important topic in behavior management is punishment, which I like to refer to as discipline. Often, when people come to my office or to a lecture to discuss behavior, they are thinking about discipline and how to *make a behavior stop!* However, discipline is really the last resort in most cases. Remember, discipline is what we call a "reactive strategy," or something that we do *after* a behavior has occurred. By that time, we have already missed an opportunity to *prevent* that behavior from occurring in the first place.

Still, there are effective ways and ineffective ways to discipline. Given that children with DS are typically quite social and responsive to social cues, it is not very effective to respond to undesirable behavior by yelling, becoming very emotional or animated, or talking. In fact, as we discussed, and given the language difficulties common in DS, the words that a caregiver says are often not important, as the person does not truly process them. What is processed instead is the strong emotions, eye contact, and facial expressions that we adults make when we are mad, even if we do not know it.

So, if we know that becoming very upset can really backfire when responding to behavior, we also have a hint as to what may work. Indeed, *taking away* the social responses for negative behaviors can be far more powerful as a form of discipline or punishment. For example, parents are often surprised when children are in my office, throwing toys, ripping papers, and being generally disruptive, yet I turn my chair, look down at my notes (removing eye contact), and do not respond at all. I often have to coach parents to follow my lead. Interestingly, while a few toys may be thrown, typically within seconds the child's behavior changes dramatically.

After a few moments, children often approach me or their parents in a calmer manner, with an inquisitive look as if to say, "That isn't getting your attention? What can I do that *will* get your attention?" At this point, I usually redirect the child to do something that is either fun ("Can you build a tower from these blocks?") or helpful ("Can you please be my helper and clean up these markers?"). And of course, when they engage in this *desired* behavior, I respond with lots of attention, including eye contact and praise. In this way, I am using myself and my own reactions as my most powerful tool in *shaping* the child's behavior. Knowing that he is seeking attention and social engagement, I am offering attention when he is engaging in positive behaviors and removing *myself* when he is engaging in negative behaviors. Discipline is discussed in more detail in chapter 8.

Chapter 4

Common Behavior Problems in Down Syndrome

So often when parents come into my office to talk about their child with DS and her behavior issues, they feel isolated and that they are failing as parents. Indeed, the frustration of managing negative behaviors can take a real toll on a family. Equally often, I am able to say to families that I have heard many, many similar stories. I relay this not to diminish the impact of behavior issues on the family, but to point out that these issues are incredibly common and widespread. So, as a reader of this book, you are by no means alone.

There are many behavior issues that are common in individuals with Down syndrome. And again, I believe that these behaviors are so widespread because of a basic mismatch of the unique neurodevelopment of individuals with DS and a world that is often not a great fit. As a result, we often see those with DS act out in very consistent ways. However, as each individual with DS is unique, we also see some less common behaviors. Here, I aim to outline some of the common and uncommon behaviors we see in those with DS and to provide some examples of each. Hopefully, this will provide a "lay of the land" and allow you, as the reader, to feel as though this book may offer some insight into the struggles you are facing.

The "Stop and Flop" and Task Refusal

The first and most commonly reported behavior challenge in people with DS is the "stop and flop." In other words, you ask your child to do something (most likely something that she does not wish to do), and she stops in her tracks and "flops" to the floor like a rag doll. Here are some common examples of this behavior:

- The birthday party is over, and Meghan has to stop playing air hockey. Stop and flop!
- It is time to get on the bus, and Jonathan does not want to go to school. Stop and flop!
- It is bedtime, and Sam does not want to stop playing with his blocks. Stop and flop!

At other times, this behavior can seem completely bizarre to a family. This can be very frustrating for families, particularly because the behavior sometimes does not seem to fit any pattern (at least, not at first). For example,

I have had countless parents report that their children will stop and flop when asked to transition to something they actually enjoy, like karate class. In one case, John, age eight, was all ready for Tae Kwon Do and even had his gi on. He loves TKD and always has a great time. However, after his father gave him his snack and asked him to come out to the car, he flopped to the floor and had a tantrum. Naturally, this left John's father feeling utterly confused and frustrated. Don't we have enough to deal with, he wondered? Why is John refusing to do something he likes!?

Once children are a bit older, their stop and flop behaviors often diminish. However, they often continue to refuse to do things they do not like. For many older children and adolescents with DS, we see what can be referred to more simply as "task refusal." That is, a parent or teacher has asked Kristen to do something, but she simply does not do it or says "No." She may not fall to the floor, but the impact is the same. The task does not get done, and the parent or teacher is frustrated.

To manage stop and flop or task refusal, we usually have to build in some motivation and focus on the future, or what's *next*. We will talk later about "if-then" statements, such as "if you come to the cafeteria, you can sit with

Maria." For other challenges, like refusing to transition, it may be a matter of building in a reward. For example, once Sarina completes all of her chores, she gets to play a computer game. Handling stop and flop or task refusal is covered in more detail in later chapters.

Elopement (Bolting)

Another behavior we see quite commonly, particularly in young children with DS, is "elopement." This is a clinical term for running off. Young children with DS may run away in public when they spot a toy or object that is interesting, run out of the classroom when a particular subject starts, or leave the house when they feel like playing outside. This is naturally quite terrifying for most parents—and for school personnel, psychologists, or other adults working with them!

While I often recommend ignoring behaviors, we cannot ignore this one, because the child could get lost or be hurt. This can be a tricky behavior to manage, particularly at first. Parents and teachers tend to become very anxious, which leads to them being upset, which leads to yelling and lots of emotion. Even though the words used to tell a child "don't do that!" are intended to stop the behavior, we know that commands may not be effective. Rather, the very fact that parents and teachers are so upset can be very reinforcing and keep the behavior going.

I have worked with many families of children with DS who are "runners," and the parents most often report that the child thinks "it's a game" and seems to enjoy being chased. Indeed, the fact that the parents are terrified and upset is not the message the child is receiving. Rather, the child is seeing that she got a *big* reaction and a lot of attention. In other words, this is fun!

And as we will discuss in far more detail later in the book, when a child runs off, it is a great time to practice how to respond...*but don't react.* For we have to catch that kid so she does not get hurt, but we have to also keep our emotions cool so we do not make the behavior fun. And of course, we have to build in strategies to prevent this from happening in the first place.

Physical Aggression

Next, psychologists have a funny habit, maybe one of many, of making simple concepts sound really complicated. For example, they have come up with the term *aggressive social problem solving.* This is more commonly known as hitting! However, it is a real problem. Very often, individuals with

Down syndrome, particularly those who have limited expressive language (speech or another reliable way of communicating their thoughts), rely on aggression to express themselves.

Indeed, many children are referred to me because they are hitting other children in their classroom. Often, it is not that the child wishes to harm anyone at all. Rather, she usually wants attention or to play but does not have the necessary language to ask appropriately. In fact, any time someone with DS has a conflict with another person and is struggling with any or all of the skills needed to manage the conflict—such as planning an approach, considering the options and their consequences, restraining her impulses, and using language to express herself—she may resort to hitting. After all, what other options does she have? Furthermore, hitting is sure to get some attention, even though it only makes matters worse. As you now know, getting attention, even if the person providing it is upset, is very reinforcing.

For behaviors like hitting, understanding the cause is the most important step of all. Is the child hitting because she wants to get some attention from a classmate, or is she frustrated by her homework? Depending on the answer, we might respond differently by helping a child learn ways to ask a friend to play, or asking the teachers to help adapt the homework assignments.

● ● ● ● ● ● ● ● ● ● ●

Stimming

Another very common behavior concern for families is "stimming." This is a shorthand term for self-stimulatory behaviors. In other words, they are behaviors that do not serve a particular function but are "self-reinforcing." That is, the behavior itself is its own reward. It simply "feels good." Some examples of stimming include flicking fingers in front of one's face; repetitively playing with objects such as by twirling a string or a rubber band; tongue clicking; teeth grinding; or flapping one's hands repetitively.

As a clinician, I usually do not worry too much about stimming. Of course, when stimming occurs very often and is accompanied by problems with socializing and communication, it may be a sign of autism spectrum disorder. However, very often, stimming occurs on its own and is not a sign of any other issue aside from developmental delays. As a pediatric psychologist who focuses on behavior, I rarely reference Sigmund Freud, the founder of psychoanalysis. However, Freud certainly got some things right. One such thing was his notion that something is only a problem if it interferes with your ability to love and to work. In other words, if it is not getting in the way of living your life, it is not a problem. I apply this concept to stimming behaviors.

We have to consider how much the behavior is happening, when, and where. If a child is stimming so much that she refuses to engage with her teacher, friends, or family, then it may be a problem. However, if a child has had a long school day and worked to the best of her ability and then chooses to come home and twirl a rubber band, this may be her way of managing and reducing stress. Think about it this way—the world is full of language, social demands, and stress. Adults can come home and read, watch a television show, or chat with a friend or family member to relax. For many children with disabilities, stimming is a very simple, and therefore relaxing, activity.

So, if stimming is not getting in the way of other things (which is crucial to determine), I encourage families to let it go and perhaps try to limit the behavior to certain times or places (e.g., after school in the bedroom). We will talk more about this in chapter 10 when discussing adolescence.

Self-Talk and Imaginary Friends

Particularly as they grow older, many children with Down syndrome engage in self-talk, and some seem to return to imaginary play. This can be concerning to families who wonder if their child is "hearing voices" or struggling to separate reality and fantasy.

While these concerns are certainly understandable and must be addressed, hearing voices or seeing things that are not really there are rare in children and adolescents with DS. What is more common is that as the world becomes a more complicated place—such as when children move to middle or high school—the day can become more stressful. Similar to stimming behaviors, engaging in self-talk and imaginary play can be a way to calm down and relax. It can also be a way to process all that has happened in a busy day. Adolescents with DS may relax by recreating scenes from a television show or movie. Or they may reenact various conversations from their school days.

Again, how to handle this behavior comes down to a matter of degree. If an individual is choosing *only* to sit alone and "script" TV shows, it may be a problem, as it is interfering with other aspects of life. However, if the person is able to be redirected and join the family for dinner after thirty minutes of "scripting," it may not be an issue after all.

Insistence on "Sameness"

Many families tell me that they think their child has OCD, or obsessive-compulsive disorder. Indeed, many people with DS have a strong desire to have everything be "just so." They may insist on sameness at home, such as insisting that everything in their bedroom be in its place with all doors and drawers closed. They may also extend this behavior to public settings, and, for example, insist that certain family members sit in certain places at a restaurant. Surely, this behavior can be frustrating, and I understand how this seems like "OCD behavior."

First, we should clarify what OCD is and is not. Like many individuals with DS, people with OCD also often like things "just so." However, OCD also usually involves very troubling thoughts. People with OCD typically believe on some level that if they do not do this particular task in a certain way, something really bad will happen. That's where the "obsessive" in OCD comes from. Of course, OCD can and does occur in people with DS. However, it is much less common than insistence on sameness and preferring predictability and order.

I find that most people with DS who become fixated on "sameness" do not have accompanying thoughts of something terrible happening. Rather, it seems that sameness makes them feel better on an emotional level. It seems to provide a feeling of security, and, maybe to a greater extent, of control. This is certainly also true for those with OCD, but, again, those thoughts of horrible things happening are really important as well.

For understanding how to deal with this type of behavior, we once again can turn back to Freud. Insistence on sameness is only a problem if it's getting in the way of someone's daily life. If Hailey cannot go to dinner with her family because she will never be happy with the seating arrangements and will act out as a result, that's a problem. But if Jackie simply asks people to sit in certain spots, but soon they all have a nice dinner regardless of whether they sit where Jackie asks, her behavior may not be a problem. Some families actively work on building in flexibility, purposefully not giving in to demands for sameness. This seems to work at times, but not always. And the individual's preference for sameness seems to remain. But we have to be careful not to actually reinforce this insistence on sameness (e.g., by always giving in to it), since it is not something we can always achieve in the real world.

Another way children and teens may show their preference for sameness is through a deep-seated dislike for transitions. Many individuals with DS have a very hard time with changes of any kind, including transitions. As we have discussed throughout the book so far, those with DS often experience the world as unpredictable, which leads to a great deal of anxiety. When a routine is established and then broken, it makes sense that an individual with DS reacts strongly and negatively. So, we have to be aware of this preference for routine, try to keep the routine, and prepare people for when that routine is going to go awry. Transitions and routines are covered in detail in later chapters.

Problems with Boundaries

Many families also come to me with concerns about their child's ability to observe boundaries. Many children with DS have difficulties learning about "stranger danger," and they can be prone to hugging strangers, or worse, willing to walk off with just about anyone. Even writing about this is scary!

If we pause for a moment and put our fears aside, we can understand this behavior. After all, this is a group of people who, on average, love other people and social attention. In addition, we know there are challenges with executive functions and controlling impulses. So of course some people with DS want to hug anyone they meet!

When children with DS are young, this behavior is managed very much by controlling the environment. We hold hands, we use strollers, and we remain vigilant. However, as children with DS mature, we can and should try to teach them skills to enable them to understand stranger danger and various types of relationships. I have worked on this issue with countless children with, you guessed it, visuals! There are also very effective programs designed for older people with disabilities that teach about relationships and boundaries. There is more on this in chapter 10, "Adolescence."

Other Behaviors

Above, I have addressed only a few of the behavior challenges that you are likely facing. The true list of all behaviors that the parent or teacher of a child or teenager with DS may observe is virtually endless. Parents and teachers face all sorts of issues from overeating to stripping clothing off in front of classmates.

I hope that the above discussion has given you a general sense of some common behavioral problems and how you can begin to understand them. Understanding gives you a giant head start for intervention. After all, if you understand a behavior, you can be thoughtful about how to respond to it. If we do not understand a behavior, we are all prone to feeling that its sole purpose is to make us nuts! When we understand a behavior, we can think about helpful ways to respond. But when we do not understand it, we tend to react, and our own behavior is driven more by emotion. And of course, when we are reacting emotionally, individuals with DS perceive that loud and clear and behavior usually worsens. This is the beginning of learning to respond… *but don't react.*

Chapter 5

A Behavior Management System Designed for Children with Down Syndrome

When we know someone has Down syndrome, we have a big head start in understanding his or her behavior. We know that, in all likelihood, some of the brain differences discussed in earlier chapters are present, and, as a result, children and adolescents with Down syndrome are likely to respond to certain types of interventions and not to others. As I have worked with more and more families, I have found that this particular system, outlined in the following pages, seems to work for many children and adolescents with Down syndrome. As they say, though, if you have met one child with Down syndrome, you have met one child with Down syndrome. That is, everyone is different, and this system may not be a good fit for all. Still, this method is based on solid behavioral principles and an understanding of the brain in Down syndrome. As a result, with some tweaks and adjustments for the individual child, I have found it to be quite successful for most families.

An important note about using this or any behavior management system is that any intervention is a constantly evolving process. That is, we have to constantly adjust and change the system to adapt to new challenges or gains. The easiest example of a change that calls for adaptation is simple maturity. As children grow and develop, their problem behaviors change, what motivates them changes, and we must change also.

With that in mind, I aim to outline my behavioral intervention system while also explaining my rationale for each portion. By so doing, I hope that I can help you, the reader, understand *why* I am suggesting a particular method. If you understand the logic, you can then be creative in adjusting the method to meet your own child's needs. Again, when I am working with families individually, I explain this by telling them, "My goal is for you to fire me." In other words, I hope to teach the principles and strategies so that families can use them on their own and adapt them as needed over time. Surely, "tune-ups" are necessary, and I often check in with families over time. However, I have also worked with countless families who simply learn the strategies and the principles underlying them and then go on to apply them so successfully that their child's behavior becomes an afterthought. And that is my goal for you.

Step 1: Maintain the Relationship

My favorite study of all time was conducted by Harry Harlow in the 1950s. At this time and for about fifty years prior, during the early years of people really studying the human mind, many scholars were focused on "drive theory." In other words, scientists believed that people only really were connected with their parents because they satisfied their basic needs, such as providing food, water, and shelter. Harlow wanted to test this hypothesis, and thank goodness he did.

Harlow worked with rhesus monkeys. He put the monkeys in cages with two "mothers," both of which were mechanical rather than their actual biological mothers. One "mother" was a monkey-shaped wire mother that provided both food and water. The other "mother" was a similar structure, but covered in soft terry cloth, and with a head that looked like a monkey's. The terry-cloth mother provided no food or water. Harlow predicted that, if drive theory were correct, then the monkeys would pay no attention to the terry-cloth mother, as it provided for none of their basic needs. However, the opposite proved to be true. The monkeys spent nearly all of their time with the terry-cloth mothers. They would grab a bite and a drink from the wire

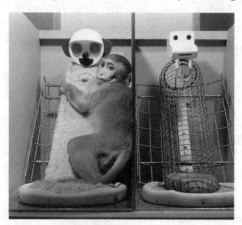

mother, but quickly scurry back to the terry-cloth mother. When they were upset, frightened, or simply relaxing, they clung to the terry-cloth mother. Harlow then concluded that there was more to the parent-child connection than meeting drives, of course. And this gave rise to "attachment theory."

Attachment theory is one of the driving forces of modern psychology. A healthy attachment to a parent or caregiver is one of the most basic elements of being alive. Further studies have shown that animals with healthy attachment are better able to regulate stress hormones and that humans do far better in all regards, socially, emotionally, and biologically, when they have a "secure" attachment.

Given these findings, I use attachment as my guiding light when working with families. I believe that the bond between caregiver and child is a sacred relationship that must be preserved above all else. Therefore, when behavior gets tough, take a step back and think about your relationship with this child. When you do not know what to do, consider what would be in the best interest of your relationship and reduce the stress on that relationship. Perhaps it means taking a break, walking away, or ignoring a behavior. Often, that might be the best strategy.

Sometimes, I tell parents to just do the complete opposite of what their instincts tell them. For example, if they are incredibly frustrated and simply want to punish as harshly as possible, I tell them to try to think of something fun to do. Often, not only does this preserve the relationship, but it also changes the "behavioral momentum." The child receives some good feedback, the parent is happier, and the child knows it. All of a sudden, things may improve on their own.

So, again, when all else fails, remember how important your relationship is with your child and focus on preserving that.

This does not mean that you should not have high expectations for your child's behavior. What we are developing here are strategies that will be most effective in improving your child's behavior over the long term. In the meantime, building the connection with your child and enjoying positive times together will help motivate him even more and ultimately lead to better behavior.

Step 2: Structure the Environment for Success

As we have discussed throughout the previous sections, there are some common brain differences in people with DS. Keeping these differences in mind gives us that "head start" I have discussed previously in thinking about behavior. We know, for example, that taking in new information, particularly verbal information, can be hard for children with DS. We also know that due to differences in the memory systems of the brain, hanging on to new information can be difficult. So, I think that every day represents seemingly new challenges for those with DS if there is not a *ton* of consistency. It is harder for them to make sense of the world, and therefore it is harder for them to predict what will be coming next.

If you imagined yourself going through life in this manner, the world would seem like a pretty scary place. I often think about this as similar to being in a foreign country where you do not speak the language. If you are being asked to do a lot of things, and people are frustrated when you do not do what they want, it can become very overwhelming, very quickly. Indeed, all of us are asked to do a great deal on any given day, and people with disabilities are often given even more direction and instructions than their peers. To make matters worse, these directions are typically given verbally, and it is not uncommon for adults to become frustrated when their instructions aren't followed at all or aren't followed quickly or well enough.

If you take a step back and view this from a big-picture perspective, you can see that we are demanding a great deal from individuals with DS, primarily using language to direct them, and becoming frustrated when they do not comply. All this, for a group of people who struggle to process language and are acutely sensitive to others' emotions. In other words, it is a recipe for disaster, and it is no surprise that so many individuals with DS exhibit behavior challenges. The environment, without some tweaking, is often not a great fit for the way their brains work.

However, all is not lost. With a bit of thoughtful consideration, we can make small changes to the environment that have a huge impact on behavior, and the underlying anxiety and well-being, of those with DS.

Perhaps the easiest and most important thing we can do for children with DS is to create routine. Routine makes the world, and day-to-day life, more predictable. In my opinion, this helps to support the challenges that those with DS face when processing lots of new information, which can be quite anxiety-provoking. It allows for the day to be predictable, thereby reducing anxiety. But how do we make a routine that is consistent, does not require us as adults to constantly direct with too much language, and is a good fit for people with DS?

Step 3: Use Visuals, Visuals, Visuals

If the rule in real estate is "location, location, location," then the rule for managing behavior for individuals with DS is "visuals, visuals, visuals." I have to admit that when I began working with children, I rolled my eyes a bit at the idea that every child seemed to need a visual aid or a visual schedule. Now, I am teased by my colleagues that nobody leaves my office without a visual schedule.

The simple reason is this: they work. Visual schedules are a very powerful thing for a few reasons. First, for children with DS, processing language is hard. Processing visuals is relatively easy. But we, as adults, rely very heavily on spoken language. When we are happy, we talk more; when we are upset, we talk more; and when children are misbehaving, *we talk a lot more.*

So, let's take the most common trigger for challenging behavior in my experience—the morning routine. For most families who come in to talk about behavior in their child with DS, I can predict the most problematic part of the day: getting out of the house. Some children may stop and flop to the floor; others strip their clothes off after their parents worked so hard to get them dressed. Still more children refuse to complete basic tasks such as brushing their teeth. As discussed above, there are motivational differences in people with DS that likely help to explain these behaviors.

But now let's think about what we do as adults. When a child is struggling to get ready in the morning, we talk. We direct him: "Brush your teeth, get your shirt on, eat this breakfast, put on your shoes..." And we do this over and over, and talk even more when he refuses. So, for me, this looks like a basic mismatch of a neurodevelopmental profile—being better at processing visuals than language—and intervention—talking more when things are not going well.

If you think back to the relationship between parent and child, you can see that the use of language to "prompt" (or maybe nag) children to do what you want to do puts incredible stress on the relationship. The parent is becoming more and more frustrated, showing lots of body language and emotion that the child can see (my mom is mad!). But the language the parent is using to try to help the situation is not being processed. So, we aren't really

getting much benefit from all the talking. On the contrary, the child is sensing that the parent is upset with him, and the parent is feeling more and more frustrated. The stress on the relationship is building, and the verbal "directions" aren't doing any good. It's a lose-lose situation.

For individuals with DS, a visual schedule not only makes the demands clear and taps a strength (visual processing) rather than a weakness (verbal processing), but it also *reduces* the overall amount of language being used. This, in my opinion, reduces the amount of cognitive stress that a child experiences. And, to boot, it decreases the stress on the relationship between child and parent. All of a sudden, there is a "third party" in the form of a visual schedule on the wall. It's not just about a parent and child struggling about the routine. There is another piece to the puzzle, and that piece can take the stress level way down.

The next benefit of a visual schedule is that it provides routine. Routine is a magical thing for us all. I complete my morning routine in the same order every day. Of course, psychologists are notoriously a bit neurotic, but I think this is pretty normal. I follow a routine because it saves time and makes the morning a little easier. I know what's coming next and how long it will take.

Because individuals with DS have a harder time with taking in new information and hanging on to it (i.e., "memory consolidation"), the world can be a much more complicated and anxiety-provoking place. One way to offset this is to provide "sameness." That is, to have things be predictable in some way. This can be accomplished by previewing, or telling individuals what is coming next, which is in itself a helpful strategy. But a visual schedule provides a structure, a preview of what's to come, and *consistency* from day to day. It makes the unpredictable world a little more predictable. I have been amazed to discover that for many children, simply having a visual schedule can completely eliminate behaviors for particular parts of the day.

The final reason (that I know of, anyhow) that visual schedules are so effective harkens back to the relationship. Consider again that language processing is so difficult for most people with DS. Yet when we adults engage with others, we rely almost exclusively upon language. As we become more frustrated with a child's behavior, we talk more, which is stressful to the child with DS. In addition, as discussed above, the child *perceives* our frustration at a very high level, which presents another stress. Thus, in this scenario, everyone loses and behavior is likely to worsen.

Introducing a visual schedule is a powerful way to reduce this stress on the caregiver-child relationship. Again, there is a third party. There is a schedule on the wall. The child or the parent can return to it with no language and less emotion. Instead of going back and forth, verbally, in what has likely turned into a power struggle, we have created a triangle (child, caregiver, schedule) to dilute some of the stress. Again, I have found this to be a surprisingly powerful way to help children get through their routines and to substantially reduce the stress on caregivers.

Making a Visual Schedule

One of the key principles of using a visual schedule is that it should make things simpler. I once worked with a lovely mother of a child with DS who came to our second visit with a visual schedule that was about twenty feet long. It was comprised of many pages taped together, and outlined every single task the child should do for the entire day. Clearly, this was my error in not providing enough guidance.

For any part of a behavior plan to be effective, it has to be simple. A good guideline for determining whether a visual schedule (or any aspect of a behavior plan) is appropriate is that the child should be able to explain it (even if through sign language or augmentative communication).

For a visual schedule, focus on a particular time of the day, and include just a few tasks that a child is capable of completing, mostly on his own. I very often suggest visual schedules for the morning and evening routines, as they are usually pretty consistent over time. This can substantially reduce the stress in a household. So, for example, for a preschool or early school-age child, a simple chart may show that he should use the potty, help with getting dressed, and eat breakfast. While he may need some help with some of these tasks, the tasks should be things he is doing mostly independently. Further, the tasks should be very clear so we know if the child did or did not complete them. For example, putting on your shirt, using the potty, and brushing your teeth are much more measurable compared to "getting ready," which is too broad and vague.

The tasks on a visual schedule should also be positive, not negative. So, we pick a "job" that the child can complete rather than a behavior we are trying to avoid such as "hands to yourself." For a younger child, a visual schedule for the morning routine may look something like this:

The Picture Communication Symbols are used with permission from Mayer-Johnson LLC

And for a slightly older child, the visual schedule may become longer and a bit more advanced in terms of jobs, but still focused on clear and discrete tasks, all positive. It may look like this:

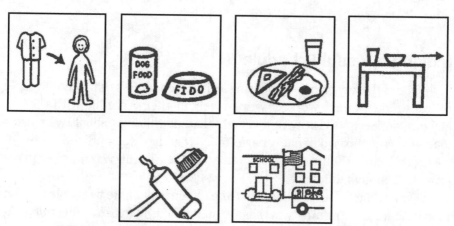

The Picture Communication Symbols are used with permission from Mayer-Johnson LLC

Some families find it helpful to take pictures of their child doing these tasks, which may help bring the schedule to life and can also be a way for the child to participate in creating the schedule. I certainly support this practice, but remember, *keep it simple*. In other words, you do not need to wait until you have a professional photo shoot with a perfect set of pictures. Do what works for you and your family, and get started!

And of course, we need to adapt over time. A young child may love moving a picture with a Velcro strip from the "Not Done" to "Done" column of a schedule. A teenager who is a great reader may choose to have a checklist, without pictures, to help with the morning or evening routine. For many families, apps on a tablet are a great choice because they allow you to easily create and manage visual schedules. Be careful, though, because you do want the schedule to be pretty consistent day to day for at least a few months, generally. So, changing the order of tasks or the tasks themselves too frequently could do more harm than good. After all, you want to gain all the benefits of establishing a new routine.

Finally, one last note about a visual schedule, particularly for certain times of the day such as the morning routine. These types of visual schedules don't just make things easier in the short term. In addition, if a child or teen with DS has years of practice using a visual schedule to follow a particular routine, by the time he reaches adulthood, that routine is likely to be very well established. And what a difference it can make for a young adult with DS to be able to wake up and complete all aspects of a morning routine on his own. That could make the difference between being able to live independently or not. So, compared to a parent running after a child and yelling at him to do this and do that, a routine with a visual schedule is really a win-win. It helps people with DS complete important tasks, reduces the stress on the relationship, and builds skills for later in life.

Step 4: Notice Good Behavior and Set Up Token Economies

Did you roll your eyes when you saw the words *token economy*? I understand if you did. After all, it certainly sounds difficult, technical, and for those who have done some behavior management before, maybe a bit cliché. And it's true, token economies are used a lot, and can be difficult to manage. However, it turns out that they are often used incorrectly, and that even with the best intentions, people often make them too complicated.

In my opinion, a token economy should be simple and easy for the family to use. After all, if a family is going to do something *consistently* over time, it has to be reasonable. It has to fit in with real life. My goal is not to put something really difficult in place that a family *must do*. Instead, the token economy should be something pretty simple that, in the end, saves time and makes life easier. But before we get to the details, I want to make sure you understand why we bother with token economies. After all, if they so often get a bad rap, are they even worth it?

Let's start by remembering that if we want good behavior to recur, we have to reinforce it. Given that many children with DS are very socially engaged, it is quite easy to reinforce good behaviors. Simply noticing these behaviors is key. However, it is well documented that when children are having behavior difficulties, adults become stressed and tend to notice far more negative behaviors than positive behaviors. This can be very disheartening for a child.

Again, think back to the example of going to work. If you went to work each day and all day long your boss told you that you were making mistakes and noticed every little thing you did "wrong," how long would it take for you to quit? Now imagine that your boss also paid no attention to the things you did correctly. Sounds like a good way to make someone anxious and miserable, right?

This is, quite often, the experience of an individual with a disability. At baseline, he is being directed what to do and how to behave all day. That's tiring in itself. Then, if we are only going to pay attention when he does things wrong and do not even notice when he does things well, we can expect that he is going to act out.

By making sure we notice the good stuff, we build in "differential reinforcement." That is, we teach children through our responses that even when things aren't going very well behaviorally, they can get some attention for doing positive things. This is crucial for long-term behavioral success. If we only notice the "bad stuff," we can quickly make children feel pretty helpless. Some children with DS have even told me that they were "bad kids" because they had received so much negative feedback. Thankfully, most children are quite resilient, and we can turn this around quickly, but only if we clearly and *consistently* notice the good stuff.

To notice good behavior, we have to be conscious of it. Adults are prone to thinking of children as just smaller versions of adults. It is not natural for us to notice little things that we "expect." So, we really have to turn up the radar for our behavioral awareness.

When noticing good behavior, it is helpful to be specific and name the behavior you like. But keep the language simple. For example, say, "Good teeth brushing" rather than "I really like how well you are brushing your teeth like a big girl." Perhaps more important than using language to show your enthusiasm for a behavior is the emotion you put into it. Showing your child that you are genuinely happy and excited about what a great job he is doing brushing her teeth with a big smile on your face will go a lot further than an old-fashioned, "Good job" with no emotion attached to it.

Noticing good behavior seems pretty straightforward, right? Of course, you could probably wake up in the morning and tell yourself, I am going to point out every good little thing my daughter does today! And, maybe you would be successful. But how long could you sustain this? What about after dinner, when you are exhausted and your child will not go to bed? What about two weeks from now, when you've forgotten how frustrated you are and things at work are stressful? We are only human, after all, and it is simply not natural to notice and point out every single good thing your child does. Without some help, most of us adults lapse and fall into the trap of noticing more bad behavior than good behavior. This is where a token economy can be a life saver.

Token Economy—The Basics

Since we cannot, and simply do not, praise our children for everything they do right, we as adults need some structure, too. This is where the token economy really shows its worth—not to the child, but to the adult. A token economy (reward system, usually a chart) is a very important and effective way to provide some positive feedback even when a child has many behavior issues. When we can provide positive feedback for the good stuff, even when there is lots of bad stuff, we start to *shape* behavior.

Just as I initially doubted the universal need for visual schedules, I was also pretty resistant to the idea that *every* child with behavior problems needs a token economy. However, over time, I have become convinced that token economies are very important for individuals with DS. To start, a token economy is not nearly as complicated as it sounds. Basically, we are picking out some things that we would like an individual to do, setting up a structure around it, and then using something that he likes and finds motivating as a reward.

One of the first things I usually hear when I suggest trying a token economy is concern that we are "bribing" the child. After all, why does he need a reward? Shouldn't this child simply *want* to behave and do positive things? For this question, I have two responses: a simple one and a more complicated one. The simple response is this: When you go to work, do you receive a reward or do you simply *want* to do a good job? Unless you are fortunate enough to be a lottery winner with no financial needs, you probably expect to be paid, or rewarded, for your work. On a very basic philosophical level, I view this issue similarly for children. Yes, they likely wish to do a "good job," whatever that means. However, defining what a good job means and providing an incentive for doing it is likely to be really helpful.

The more complicated answer to the question above involves revisiting the brain in DS. Remember, motivation is an area of difference, and individuals with Down syndrome can sometimes exhibit reduced "task mastery." That is, they may become more frustrated and struggle to fully complete a task. Brain differences are certainly part of this. But I believe that simply running out of gas—or mental energy, as discussed in chapter 2—is a major factor as well. With that in mind, I think it is important to build external structures to motivate children with DS. Doing so helps to support a neurodevelopmental difference, and it's a win-win—children are more successful, parents are less frustrated, and there is less stress on the relationship.

An added benefit or bonus of a token economy is that you can use it as a tool for redirection when things are going poorly. For example, let's say that your child is starting to act out (for example, jumping on his sister's bed) because he wants some attention. You might point to the token economy/job chart and direct him to complete one of his jobs. He can then earn a reward and avoid a negative behavior and a possible punishment.

Making a Token Economy

Perhaps even more than with visual schedules, people can fall into a lot of traps with token economies. The first trap is the "do-nothing" trap. Often, people hear the term *token economy* and, in their minds, run out of my office door, even as they sit and listen to me. It is an intimidating term that sounds much fancier than it needs to. Do not be afraid—you too can make a token economy, and it shouldn't take more than a few minutes.

The next trap that people fall into with token economies is the same one we discussed for visual schedules. People often get a little too fancy. Again, I have worked with many families who return to my office with very complex token economies that all members of the family struggle to understand. To make matters worse, plenty of books suggest setting up very complex token economies that use point systems, gaining or losing points all day long (i.e., contingency systems), and noticing every small behavior, good or bad. In my opinion, a complex behavior plan, and therefore token economy, is not usually a good behavior plan, particularly for those with Down syndrome.

I prefer to keep things simple. Similar to how Steve Jobs viewed Apple products, I believe that the best way to make something effective is to make it simple and user friendly. In other words, if you really understand something, such as behavior, you should be able to address it in a simple manner. So, while it takes some time to understand the logic behind these methods (or, perhaps, the "method behind the madness"), the actual implementation should be pretty straightforward. With that in mind, my token economies are notoriously simple. Here are my guidelines for creating an effective token economy.

1. The chart should be simple, with only a few tasks.

Again, complex does not mean effective. Start slow, with about three or four jobs for a particular time of the day (e.g., morning routine). Make sure these are tasks that can be done in a relatively short amount of time so that the child can earn a reward of some kind pretty quickly. Developmentally, this allows the child to understand the connection between doing positive things and being rewarded. This reinforces the behavior and makes it more likely to keep happening.

Take care not to set up a system in which the reward happens too far in the future, such as having "good behavior" all day long to earn a prize at the end. Think about it—is this child going to think at 8:00 a.m. that he had better put his shoes on quickly so that he can play with her iPad at 3:00 p.m.? That is quite a long time to wait for a reward, and you are probably losing the reinforcing effect. Best to keep it simple and quick. Young children should start their "jobs" and receive their rewards within thirty minutes maximum, ideally even less. As children mature, they can do more jobs and wait longer for rewards. An adolescent, for example, may be able to work all day for a reward when he gets home from school. But again, be careful and make sure that the behaviors and the rewards are connecting for the individual.

2. The child must understand how the system works.

This is a good test of whether a behavior plan is developmentally appropriate. If a child does not understand his token economy, how effective can it be? I have often met with families and seen behavior plans with token economies created at home or at school that are so complex the child has no idea how it works. Remember that you are trying to help *teach* this child *how* to behave at his best, so devising a plan that is too complex for him to understand is a tough way to start.

When I create a new token economy for a child, I almost always involve him in the process. I ask him what jobs he does at home, and which ones he wants to learn. Some children can answer verbally, while others may need to sign, use an augmentative communication device, or answer with help from a parent. Regardless, I want *some* input from the child. For a child who has less ability to communicate, the parent might pick some jobs but let the child choose the pictures for the chart.

3. The token economy must focus on POSITIVE things that the child is ABLE to do.

So, I often call a token economy a "chore chart" or "job chart."

If you remember that the chart should only include things your child is able to do, it can help keep you from falling into the trap of choosing negative

behaviors on which to focus. More often than not, I encounter token economies that include goals such as "no hitting," "calm hands," "wait my turn," and the like.

Remember reviewing the basics of behavior earlier? We want to reinforce what we want to see more of and not reinforce the behaviors we want to go away. And we know that calling attention to a behavior is, in itself, highly reinforcing, particularly for those with DS. So, it does not make sense to create a behavior plan that calls a child's, his parent's, or his teacher's attention to a behavior we are trying to get rid of. Why point out to a child that he did not hit anyone for the last ten minutes? That simply reminds him about hitting. And, of course, when he does hit, he receives a lot of feedback and attention when he does *not* earn his star, point, or other token.

Again, I think it is crucial that we focus on *positive things that we want a child to do.* As an example, for a morning routine, I return to our visual schedule above. I would like a child to help with some basic tasks in the morning such as dressing, washing up, and eating breakfast. Parents and teachers often ask me if it is acceptable to put jobs in a token economy that a child or teenager is already doing. The answer: of course! Not only are these positive behaviors that we want to reinforce by paying attention to them, but they are also really important skills. So, there is no harm, and lots of benefit, to adding structure around them and reinforcing them. After all, an adult with a disability who is able to move seamlessly through his morning routine with no help is likely to be far more independent than a peer who cannot do this. Further, we know that people with DS tend to do really well with repetition of tasks over time. So, if the individual can practice certain routines for many years, while we also build up positive behavioral momentum and create a supportive behavioral environment, we are accomplishing multiple goals at once.

At this point, you may be asking yourself what the difference is between a visual schedule and a token economy. The difference is in the reward, discussed below. You may also be asking if you need one or both of these. I prefer to have both and to use a visual schedule for an easier time of the day with a token economy (including a reward) for a more challenging time of day. For example, you may create a visual schedule for the morning routine and a token economy for the hours after school until bed, or vice versa.

4. Pick appropriate rewards, if any at all.

When I am creating behavior plans with families, choosing rewards frequently becomes a challenge and also the source of some funny stories. One very well-meaning and motivated family, for instance, had the idea of taking a trip to Six Flags every time their child completed all of his jobs. While it would be highly motivating to go to Six Flags every day, it is not likely sustainable. Other times, families are very focused on rewarding the child with some material item such as toys or stickers. While these types of rewards can be quite motivating at first, their effectiveness tends to wear off over time.

Thus, when picking rewards for a child, it is very important to consider these questions:

1. Is this realistic and sustainable (i.e., can you afford it) over time?
2. Is this going to be motivating for the long haul?
3. Is this something that the child can go without? It is tempting to use rewards such as food that are highly motivating, but probably not a good idea for the long term.

One "trick of the trade" is to pick activities and social rewards rather than material rewards. It is often quite effective to pick an activity as a reward, as this is something that a child is likely to continue to enjoy over time. One great example that I encountered involved a boy who virtually always refused to complete his evening routines. However, he really loved the TV show *Cash Cab*. We created a simple chart with his three or four jobs for nighttime, and the reward was to watch an episode of *Cash Cab* before bed. His parents were amazed that after they built in this reward, he would do *almost any-*

thing to earn it. It is very important to note that this child had been allowed to watch *Cash Cab* prior to this behavior plan. His parents did express some concern that they were now going to require some "work" from him before he could do this activity. In my experience, however, as long as the "jobs" are positive and the child attains good feedback, he or she almost never complains about the preferred activity becoming a reward. It's all about keeping things positive.

Some other examples of activities that could be used as a reward include:

- Choosing a TV show
- Playing with a favorite toy
- Playing outside
- Spending a set amount of time on the computer or iPad
- Swinging
- Blowing bubbles with a parent

In addition to activities, perhaps the most effective rewards over time for people with DS are *social* rewards. Again, if we return to the way the brain works in people with DS, we know that social cues are perceived very keenly and that social feedback is very powerful. So, when we are trying to encourage behaviors by rewarding them, we can "go back to the social well." If we can make a reward interactive in some way, a child is likely to be highly reinforced and his behavior is likely to continue to occur. Many parents choose rewards such as playing a game with a family member, reading a book with mom or dad, playing catch with a sibling, or the like. These rewards are easy to sustain over time, are highly effective, and continue to build on the relationship—which, you may recall, is the most important piece of all.

Some effective social rewards include:

- Playing a game with a family member
- Reading a book of the child's choosing with a family member
- Visiting a neighbor
- Visiting a special friend or teacher in another classroom
- Taking a walk with a friend or teacher

- Being Mommy or Daddy's helper after dinner
- Playing outside, such as catch, with a parent or sibling
- Dancing with a parent or sibling
- Making a craft together with a friend or parent
- Watching a sports event or movie on TV with a parent

As indicated by the heading of this section, which says "if any at all," the actual rewards are really not what is most important about a token economy. So often, families are most concerned about the rewards and spend a lot of time creating them. However, in countless cases I have seen, the child does not seem to be concerned about the reward. Rather, he loves that people are noticing what a good job he is doing. In other words, it is the *attention* that is really motivating him. So, while picking an effective and sustainable reward is very important, don't lose sleep over this. Remember that noticing your child's good behavior is most important and that it is really the relationship that is driving everything.

And now you are ready to make your token economy! To review, you are going to pick a few jobs that are *positive*, that happen during a relatively brief time of day, and for which your child or adolescent can earn a reward.

Designing Your Token Economy

For young children, I usually like to use token economies after school, in the afternoon and early evening. In the morning, I often rely on a visual schedule and focus on building a routine. In the afternoon and evening, I want the family to be working together to build some of that positive behavioral momentum. Don't worry about making your behavior chart look fancy. A piece of construction paper with some pictures of your child doing positive things is fine. I often rely on the computer and my basic word processing program, because I'm not very artistic. You can also use apps that are affordable and available for most devices. For a young child with DS, a token economy for after school might look something like this:

Hang coat	Put away shoes	Feed dog	Prize
✓	✓		

For an adolescent or even a young adult, I might make the chart more complicated. I might add some jobs, or I might make the length of time it takes to earn a prize longer. So, for a teen who has some really good skills around the house, I might try something like this:

Hang coat		✓
Outside time		✓
Set dinner table		
Help Dad with cooking		
Clear dishes		
Wash up for bed		
Prize		

And for an older adolescent or young adult who can understand earning rewards for longer-term efforts, I might recommend building a much more advanced system. It does not need to be complicated, but we may agree that he needs to complete everything on his chart a certain number of times to earn a reward. For example, he might need to earn twenty "stars" or tokens in order to earn a trip to the mini-golf course with his aunt. We could put this agreement up on a piece of paper on the wall or put a jar in his room and give him a special token (e.g., a shell, a special type of coin, or a marble) to drop in every time the jobs are done. If this person has some pretty good reading skills, perhaps the system does not even need to be visual but could instead be a basic checklist. Still, I prefer visuals because they are typically more powerful for those with DS. Thus, for an older adolescent or young adult, the token economy might look like this:

Clean bedroom	✓
Exercise on treadmill	
Set dinner table	✓
Clean up dinner table	✓
Do homework	
Bedtime cleanup	
Fun TV show time!	

As you can see from the above examples, my version of a token economy is nothing fancy. Token economies are not difficult to make, and they should not be difficult to do, either. Again, when we keep things simple, we have the best chance of *actually using the techniques*. So, don't be afraid of token economies. Remember, it's just what we psychologists do: we make something pretty simple sound much more complicated.

Step 5: Use Proactive Strategies to Prevent Negative Behaviors and Support Positive Behaviors

Throughout this book, you have learned a lot about how the brain works in those with Down syndrome. As GI Joe used to say, "Knowing is half the battle." When we understand why something is happening, we can be much more effective in intervening—or even preventing it in the first place. To encourage good behaviors and limit negative ones, we can again turn back to the brain and focus on what works and what does not.

Watch Your Language

Perhaps the most important thing we can do as adults is to be aware of our own language. As we discussed earlier, those with Down syndrome often understand more than they can express. However, there are limitations to language comprehension (receptive language). More complex aspects of language, such as grammar and syntax, can be hard for those with DS to understand. For example, you might tell someone with DS, "The cat was followed by the dog." Because this sentence is relatively complicated, the person might have trouble answering a question such as "Who was following whom?"

Unfortunately, when adults interact with children, they tend to use complicated language. Consider Thomas, who just whacked his sister after she refused to give him a turn on the computer. His father responded by saying (with an angry tone, of course), "Now Thomas, there is no hitting in this house! You are in big trouble. Go to your room until you are ready to apologize!"

To an adult, the message is pretty clear. Thomas broke a rule, his father is angry with him, and he is being punished. But the words Thomas's father used are pretty complicated. And when we use language that is so complex, our message is often lost. Even worse, because Thomas is likely to be really talented at reading emotions and enjoys getting a rise out of his dad, his father's reaction may actually seem exciting to him. So, giving Thomas an animated lecture on his behavior really presents a lose-lose scenario. Thomas's father's message is lost and therefore ineffective. And even worse, Thomas may actually find this emotional and strong response reinforcing. That is, it may make him more likely to repeat that behavior again! Thomas's poor dad can't catch a break.

The good news is that we can adjust our language relatively easily. For example, Thomas's father could calmly say, "No hit. Go to your room." The other information in his message is really irrelevant. This is the "meat and potatoes" of what he wants to say. A good guideline is to consider what the child can repeat back to you and clearly understand. Often, I like to think of a child's developmental level and base my language on that. A quick shortcut (that is by no means perfect but does give us a general idea of how to structure our own speech) is that if a child is at the two-year developmental level, we should use phrases of up to two words, and if a child is at the three-year developmental level, we should use phrases of up to three words, and so on. Note that I am not talking about the actual *age* of the child, but rather his developmental level, and therefore how much he understands.

So, whenever we are interacting—whether it is a neutral time, a time when we are noticing good behavior, or a time when we are managing negative behavior—we have to be aware of our own language and stick to the most important points. If we can do this effectively, all of our messages will be more effective. Surely, there is a time and place to practice more complex language. But when we are trying to manage or shape behavior, that complex language usually does more harm than good.

Focus on the Positive and the Future

Many of us are very hard on ourselves and other people. We do a great job remembering negative events that occurred in our lives, and we hang on to our emotions that occurred during those events. For some reason, probably to help us survive back when we were cave people, we humans tend to hang on to negative feelings and memories far more effectively than positive ones. Of course, if a lion chases you and bites your arm, it's good that the next time you see a lion you are completely terrified and run away. That negative emotion is serving a purpose! But this memory of negative emotions carries over to behavior as well. As we discussed before, research has clearly shown that adults notice a lot more of the negative behavior from children and often do not notice the positive behavior.

Think about what this would mean for a child. He might think, every time I screw up, my dad notices! But if I do something great, he doesn't. Of course, we cannot blame this dad. We can all relate to this dad. We have to remain aware of our own reactions and emotions and keep them in check to avoid sending the wrong message.

When interacting with individuals with DS, it is even more important to be aware of and try to control our emotions. As we learned in chapter 3, children with Down syndrome are often exquisitely sensitive to other people and their emotions. So, if we react negatively to their behaviors, they are receiving and processing that feedback very clearly. And if we are focusing on the negative behaviors, children are likely to begin to believe they are "bad" and even to exhibit negative behavior. Why wouldn't they? If I'm a "bad kid," I might as well try out some bad behaviors! Again, this takes us back to that idea of "negative behavioral momentum." In other words, a child has engaged in lots of negative behaviors and has received lots of negative reactions. That becomes familiar to the child, and he continues to act out that pattern.

But there is some good news. Children and teens with DS also are very talented at processing positive emotions and positive responses. So, as discussed earlier, that negative behavioral momentum can easily turn to positive behavioral momentum. And the power to shift this momentum lies within us, the adults, and the environment. If we can provide structure, focus on the positive, and look toward the future, children with DS tend to respond very well.

Redirect Problem Behavior When Possible

Redirection is a pretty simple but very effective strategy. When you see a child or teen begin to engage in a negative behavior, or you think that behavior may be about to start, you introduce a new idea of something to do. As you may have guessed, I usually like to make this positive and social. For example, you might notice that Madison is becoming frustrated as she waits her turn to use the tablet, and you think she is about to take a swing at her brother. To redirect her, you may say, "Madison, could you be my special helper and mix this cookie dough?" Or, "Madison, can you come show me that dance you learned at dance class again?" You have, quickly and easily, given Madison a new idea and changed the direction of her behavior.

I particularly like to ask older children and teens for help with something I need to do. As we have discussed, this allows the new behavior to be social and interactive (helping me out), and it also is likely to lead to a genuinely happy response from the adult. So now, all of a sudden, instead of a negative behavior and a negative emotional reaction from an adult, we have started a positive behavior and can respond with genuine excitement!

For young children who cannot understand these types of spoken directions, we can use simpler forms of redirection. For example, let's take a look at Amelie, age three, who is throwing toys onto the floor and looking for attention from her mother. Rather than asking Amelie to help with a job around the house, her mom chooses to bring over Amelie's favorite pop-up toy. With an excited tone of voice and enthusiastic expression, she shows Amelie how fun the toy can be. When Amelie starts to play with the toy, her mother claps and smiles. All of a sudden, Amelie goes from throwing toys onto the floor to playing with a fun toy. And to boot, she is receiving positive feedback from her mother. It's a win-win!

Step 6: Manage Difficult Situations Before They Happen

Often, children have fears of particular situations such as going to the doctor or dentist, getting a shot, or going to a new school. The same is true for those with Down syndrome, and this fear may even be amplified. If we think back to the way the brain develops for this group of people, taking in new information and holding on to it is more difficult. So, this can make the world seem like a scary place—things often seem new and uncertain. And none of us does well with uncertainty.

Fear is not just linked to uncertainty for people with DS. It is also about the emotions tied to a place or an event. For example, think about a visit to a doctor's or dentist's office or a hospital. These settings are places where children have often been poked, prodded, and, most likely, scared. For those with DS in particular, these emotionally charged events and situations are strongly embedded. But there is probably not much language tied to the events. When people work with children who have been traumatized, terms such as "preverbal" or "in the bones" are often used. This simply means that the child felt the traumatic experience at a level beyond what he could understand or make sense of at the time. If you consider a toddler who needs to have vaccine shots, you know that you cannot explain to him why the doctor has to hurt his arm. He cannot understand the benefits of the vaccine, the reason it has to hurt, and why it is ultimately worthwhile. He simply feels the pain, and that is what he remembers, on a very deep level without much meaning attached to it.

Children and teenagers with DS often have a great deal of exposure to doctors and hospitals early in life. They are often poked, prodded, and even operated on. And these experiences are often processed at that "preverbal" level discussed above. Children do not understand the context, and they cannot understand the complex reasons why this painful experience is worth it and will prevent worse experiences in the future. As a result, when children with DS have experienced lots of pain or poking and prodding by doctors, it is no surprise that they do not want to return to a doctor's office.

In addition, there is the added challenge that *talking about* the doctor's office visit is not likely to help many children with DS. Remember, language processing can be very challenging, and the major points may not be understood.

I have worked with many families who are trying to prepare a child or adolescent with DS for what is likely to be a difficult experience. The family, with the best intentions, will talk the child through what is going to happen. Often times, this leads the child to ask more and more questions, even the same ones over and over again. It is as if the information is not being processed—it probably is not!

Working in a hospital, I also often see what happens next. The child comes to the hospital for something simple, like having some blood drawn, and his anxiety is through the roof. After all, he's been hearing about it for weeks. I have encountered this more times than I can count. It seems that, while the child was likely anxious about any type of "doctor's visit," talking about what is coming next made it worse. By the time the child arrives to have his blood drawn, he may be so anxious that he refuses to even get out of the car.

We have to ask ourselves what the problem is with this scenario. When most of us are anxious, having someone talk with us about the event helps to calm us down. We psychologists call this "previewing," and it is generally a very good strategy to help manage and reduce anxiety around coming events.

So, why does this previewing technique not work so well for children and adolescents with DS? Once again, we have to return to the brain and the way people with DS, on average, process and learn new information. Here, the big issue with previewing in the typical sense is *language*.

Try to put yourself in the shoes of someone with DS. Pretend for a moment that you are again in a foreign country where you do not speak the language. Let's say you are in the outskirts of Japan, where nobody speaks English (apologies to those readers who do, in fact, speak Japanese!). Now let's pretend that you have a medical issue—perhaps your leg is turning bright red and is painful. The people of the town are very kind and helpful and bring you to the doctor's office to have this checked. The doctor is also very kind, but you cannot understand a word she is saying! The doctor begins to remove some sharp instruments and explains, in Japanese, what she is going to do to your leg. However, you have no idea what she is trying to explain.

Now, imagine on a scale of 1 to 10, how terrified you would be. Sure, this doctor is most likely going to do something that is helpful. But, how painful will it be? What is she trying to accomplish? What is the actual problem she is trying to fix? What would your own doctor suggest if she were available? What will your leg be like after this unfamiliar doctor is done?

I cannot predict how others would react, but even as I'm describing this scenario, it is making me nervous! If I had to quantify it, I would say my anxiety would be 9 out of 10. I really need that leg, after all.

This is a good example of how it feels for children and adolescents with DS to be scared of a new situation. Sure, all sorts of people appear to be nice and to know what to do, but that does not mean that the person with DS understands what is going to happen or agrees with it.

Now, let's return to that situation and pretend the Japanese doctor had a different approach. Let's say that when she realized you did not speak the same language, she pulled out some pictures or illustrations. The illustrations explained that your leg had a small infection. The next picture showed a small cut that would be made in your leg. The next picture showed a couple of stitches and a small bandage. Then there was a picture of some cream being put on the leg. And finally, and most importantly, there was a picture of a happy person who was feeling much, much better.

After seeing those pictures, you would really understand what is coming next. You would know what the problem is, generally. You would know what the doctor is planning to do with her knife, and you would know the planned outcome—feeling better with just a couple of stitches.

What is your anxiety level now, on a scale of 1 to 10? Maybe the situation is still scary, but I would guess your anxiety is under 5, and that you are looking forward to feeling better rather than being terrified of what is about to happen.

For many children with DS, difficult experiences occur very much in this way. There is clearly a sense that *something is about to happen*. Perhaps people are asking the child, "Are you ready for the doctor?" But all he may process is "DOCTOR!" Further, if the child's parent or caregiver knows that seeing the doctor has been a difficult experience in the past, there may be lots of body language and "signals" from adults.

As explained earlier, people with DS often have an incredible "social-emotional radar." So, if a parent is nervous about a doctor's visit or about how his or her child with DS will behave during that visit, this parent is likely showing his anxiety in his body language. Maybe he is being quieter and less playful than usual. Maybe he is being a little more stubborn than usual with the morning routine. We all have these subtle shifts in our behavior based on how we are feeling.

The tricky part when interacting with people with DS is that they are often quite skilled at reading body language. Whenever I begin working with a new child and her family, I ask about strengths. Very often, families report that their children with DS can "read people" exceptionally well.

This makes the job of parenting—or being a teacher, doctor, therapist, or any other adult interacting with an individual with DS—quite challenging. We often cannot use the tool that we rely on most to communicate and manage situations—our language. And on top of that, our facial expressions, tone of voice, and body language are being sensed at a very sensitive level. In other words, this is a tough job!

Thankfully, there are some tools that can help us manage these difficult situations. Remember, based on how the brain works in DS, there are some strategies that really help individuals process new information, be ready for situations, and reduce anxiety. These include using visuals, structure, and routine or predictability.

So, how can we make new and scary situations visual, structured, and predictable? It sounds pretty daunting. However, there is a technique that accomplishes these goals and it is fairly simple yet very effective—the Social Story. Social Stories are simple picture books, with relatively few words (if any), that show what will be occurring, in sequence, with the desired behaviors and outcomes. The kind Japanese doctor discussed above used what is basically a Social Story to explain to her patient what was wrong, what was going to happen, and the outcome.

The Basics of Social Stories

The Social Story is a type of visual support that was developed by Carol Gray, originally for use in helping children with autism understand the social expectations related to specific situations. But Social Stories can also be very

useful for people with Down syndrome or for any other visual learners.

Social Stories offer a simple way of adding visuals, structure, and predictability to a new event. They are simple picture books that can be made of any material you wish. I often use construction paper and photos taken with a smartphone. The book shows an event, in sequence, and relates what will happen in pictures. It also shows what the individual will be asked to do and how he is expected to behave during the event.

A Social Story should include very few words, if any. Again, the point is for it to be visual. A few words are okay, so long as the individual using the Social Story can understand them. The Social Story should include the sequence of events so that an individual knows what to expect. It is also best to have pictures that show people who are smiling and feeling positive about the experience. As stated above, the Social Story should show what we *want* to happen. What are the behaviors we would like to see? Just as with our visual schedules and token economies, we would never want to show behaviors we *do not* want to see. For example, in a Social Story about going to the doctor's office, we would show a cooperative little girl having her checkup, not a crying little boy kicking his doctor!

Pictured on page 58 is a Social Story about sleep studies. This is a relatively intensive medical procedure in which the person has to sleep overnight in the hospital, attached to many cables and with people monitoring him. This procedure was very upsetting and scary for many of our patients with Down syndrome at Boston Children's Hospital. On countless occasions, parents tried to prepare their children with DS as best they could—by talking with them about what would happen. And quite often, the child's anxiety would build and build leading up to the sleep study. By the time they arrived at the hospital, many of our patients would not comply, ripped the cords away, and stayed up the entire night. The children left feeling very upset and traumatized, and all of that effort was wasted.

Eventually, our program decided to practice what we preach and to get ahead of the game with a Social Story. As pictured below, members of our team created a simple picture book with the sequence of events and some simple language about sleep studies. And while many children still struggle with sleep studies, we seem to do a lot better when they are prepared with a Social Story. Instead of walking into a totally unfamiliar, and therefore scary, situation, they are prepared and know exactly what is going to happen. They know what is expected of them. And when people know what is coming, they are less anxious. And when they are less anxious, they tolerate the procedures far more easily.

How to Make a Social Story

1. Pick a specific event (visiting the doctor or dentist, moving to a new home, starting a new school).
2. Start at the beginning and break the story down into small steps. Use the first person (pronouns *I* or *we*) for the narration. For example: "I get in the car. Then I play with my tablet. We park at the garage."
3. Identify the desired behaviors. What do you want the person reading the Social Story to do at each step?
4. To illustrate the story, take some pictures or find some online. If possible, get some pictures of the actual building or room where the event will occur and the key people the child will be interacting with.

My friendly helper will measure my head.

My Sleep Study

My Sleep Study

5. Try to include pictures of the actual person, or someone else, feeling happy and relaxed.

6. Show the desired outcome. What will happen at the end of the event? Will you go home, go out for lunch?

7. If you choose, show a reward or prize that can be earned at the end of the event. This does not have to be something fancy or expensive. Playing a favorite game with a friend or family member, watching a favorite show or movie, or going to a favorite playground is often more than enough of an incentive.

8. Keep it *simple*. The story should not be too long, include too many words, or be expensive to make. The simpler the better. Remember, a good rule is that the person reading the book should be able to explain it to you.

9. Read the story together with the person many times, over a long period such as two to four weeks before the event. Often, I encourage families to read the story with their child at night when settling down (although maybe not as the last story before bed).

Chapter 6

Brothers and Sisters

As you have been reading through this book, I hope you have noticed that I have written a great deal about how we, the adults, can adjust our style and behavior to meet the needs of people with DS and improve their behavior. As adults, we can ask this of ourselves. We can reflect upon our own behavior and ways of managing situations and then adjust based on new information or ideas we have learned.

But, what about other children? Is it fair, reasonable, or even possible to require other children to adjust their own behavior and reactions to fit the needs of a brother or sister who learns differently? Often, when I work with families, we begin by adjusting the behavior of adults, and it tends to work quite well. But, after we see some improvement, I very often encounter questions about siblings and classmates. The adults can learn quickly and can *try* to change their behavior based on our conversations. But naturally, it is harder for other children to do so.

We have to consider the needs of other children when we ask them to adjust their own behavior and reactions to meet the needs of a sibling or a peer. Quite simply, what's in it for them? Some parents may argue, "My kids should do this because I said so!" But I have found that to be a pretty ineffective technique. It may work for a short period, but it is not likely to continue to work over the long term. And we know consistency is key.

As a psychologist, I think a lot about behavior, and behavior often boils down to incentives. Again, what's in it for me? As discussed earlier, most of us do not go to work and expect to do a good job for nothing in return. We expect to be paid for our work. While we do not need to pay siblings or classmates for managing their reactions to a child with Down syndrome, we do need to offer some incentives.

For siblings and in a home setting, we often start with a family meeting. I provide some education about the things we have discussed so far. I talk with siblings about their reactions to behavior and explain that what they say is not nearly as important as how they say it, or their body language. We often do some role playing to demonstrate how their strong reactions to negative behaviors can make those behaviors really fun and exciting for their brother or sister with DS. It is often very interesting and eye-opening for siblings to learn about this. And very often, with a little guidance, they reach the conclusion that they should try to ignore a lot of behaviors themselves. This is in an important point. You might want to stop reading here and run to your other child or children, and explain to them why they should not react so strongly to their sibling with DS. But, hold off, for now. Read a little further and think about how to have this conversation.

Typically, people are most receptive to new ideas when they come up with them on their own. So, when you do feel ready to talk with your other children, ask them what they think. For example, you might ask, "Why does Paul throw your toys all over the floor? What's in it for him? What do you think would help him stop doing this?" You may be surprised that with some targeted questions, your other children can probably figure a lot of this out. So, don't just tell them the answer, help them reach it on their own.

At this point, I hope you can take my word for it that helping siblings understand the behavior issues of their brother or sister with Down syndrome is not so difficult. However, helping them to manage their reactions to behavior is much more difficult. Thankfully, siblings of people with disabilities are often a pretty impressive group of people. I frequently encounter children who are strikingly mature and intelligent. Many siblings will take on a "parent role" and respond to their brother or sister with DS in a very adult manner. This, of course, has its benefits and its drawbacks. But with regard to behavior, siblings of individuals with DS are often willing and ready to try things that will be helpful. And I am always sure to point out that this should be helpful to them, too. We have to be careful not to make siblings feel as if this is their responsibility and that their brother or sister's needs are more important than their own.

The most daunting thing we ask of siblings is to ignore the negative behaviors of their brother or sister with DS. It is really the parents' and teachers' job to provide the external supports such as token economies and Social Stories. Siblings are primarily responsible for ignoring some things that are, frankly, hard to ignore.

Let's return for a moment to Christopher, the boy with DS who loves to jump on his sister's bed. You recall that when he did this, his sister, Morgan, became very upset. She often yelled at him to stop and cried, and her body language showed how stressful this was for her. And of course, her reactions are what made this behavior so fun for Christopher. Like many brothers (this author included, who has two older sisters with many war stories...), Christopher loves getting a rise out of his sister. So, we may be able to explain to Morgan that getting upset only makes Christopher enjoy this behavior more. She may even understand that. But when she gets home and he is jumping on her bed, sending her favorite stuffed animals flying across the room, will she really change her reaction? In my experience, no. And over time, she is even less likely to ignore this behavior without some support and an incentive.

If we want Christopher's behavior to change, we have to also address his sister's response to the behavior. Even though siblings may be somewhat selfless and mature beyond their years, we have to remember that they are still, in fact, children. And like any other human being, siblings respond best to structure and incentives. So, how can we create an incentive and some structure to help a brother or sister ignore a sibling's behavior? For me as a behaviorist, this is a bit of a mind-bending problem. How do we reward a child for *not* exhibiting a behavior, such as a response to a brother or sister who is acting out?

The first step is setting up a structure, or a set of rules/guidelines, and then to find a way to offer an incentive. Once the sibling understands the idea of ignoring a bad behavior, we have to place a structure and incentives around ignoring. Let's return to Christopher and his sister, Morgan.

When I met with the real-life family and talked with Morgan, with some pretty simple guidance, she was able to determine that her strong reactions to Christopher's jumping were probably pretty fun for him. And, fairly quickly, she reached the conclusion that not reacting, or ignoring, would probably help Christopher stop this behavior. But, she also felt that this was not fair! Why should she ignore him messing up her bed? She is a kid too, after all.

I then asked Morgan if she would like to be acknowledged, or noticed, by her parents when she ignored Christopher's behavior. She immediately brightened up. "Yes," she said, sounding a bit righteous. And in my opinion, she was right. Morgan should receive feedback for this very positive and helpful behavior, just as Christopher would for good behaviors.

We talked about some things that she likes— going out for ice cream, having special time with a parent (without Christopher), and going to the movies. Next, we came up with a plan. We agreed to put a small jar in her bedroom with some pennies nearby. Each time she successfully ignored Christopher when he jumped on her bed, she could simply put a penny in the jar. When she filled the jar, her parents would give her one of her prizes—going out for ice cream, special time with a parent, or a trip to the movies. It is important to point out that we created this plan based on what Morgan could understand and manage developmentally. As she's a bit older than Christopher, she could understand, and tolerate, working for a bit longer to earn a bigger reward. For children who are younger or have a disability, that waiting could be really difficult, if not impossible.

Morgan and her family tried out this approach for a few weeks. Christopher jumped on her bed the day after we met. Instead of reacting, she left the room and played a game on the computer. Within less than a minute, Christopher stopped jumping on her bed. A few minutes later, she marched into her room and dropped a penny in her jar, with a big smile on her face. Now let's take a step back and consider how this played out from a few different angles. First, Christopher did not get any feedback for his behavior. And sure enough, when we met a month later, he had stopped jumping on his sister's bed altogether. The behavior had been eliminated without punishment, and quickly.

The situation had greatly improved from Morgan's perspective, too. Rather than being upset when Christopher jumped on her bed, becoming upset afterward that their parents were not keeping him out of her room, and then being upset afterward because there was conflict in the home, she was now left feeling happy, successful, effective, and even rewarded! She spent almost no time being upset. Morgan was feeling pleased with her parents for noticing her good behavior, even though they did not spend any energy managing the situation.

Christopher may have lost a fun activity— making his sister upset. But there is now much less tension between him and his sister, and in the house as a whole. Now that he doesn't receive attention for this negative behavior, he is far more likely to look to his family members for positive feedback, such as by completing one of his household jobs from his token economy. In short, everyone in the household is happier and there is less stress on the system. We have managed the behavior and spared the relationships. And this, of course, will benefit everyone involved.

Of course, as siblings get older, they might have to actually deal with some of the behaviors they are seeing instead of simply ignoring them. Just as with parents, I try very hard to avoid siblings having to punish one another. So, I usually would *not* encourage a brother or sister to give a time-out or other punishment to their sibling with DS. But that does not mean they cannot use some other strategies. Siblings can absolutely redirect their brother or sister with DS to do something more positive. They can distract from a negative behavior, and they can remind their sibling of their jobs around the house and ways to receive positive feedback and attention. So, use your good judgment as a parent to decide when to ask your other child or children to help out with behavior. But remember, keep it positive and help them respond... *but don't react.*

Handling Sibling Conflicts in Your Home

I hope that you can understand the concept underlying the above example of Christopher and Megan and adapt it to fit your children's and family's situation. You do not have to use an ignoring jar with a trip for ice cream as a reward. Rather, I hope you understand *why* this strategy was so effective. We set up a structure—Morgan understood that Christopher wanted a reaction from her, that her reaction was driving the behavior, and that her parents wanted to reward her for *not* giving the reaction.

In your household, you may have older children who just need to understand the process but do not need a reward. Or you may have a younger child who needs a more immediate reward. Regardless of these factors, what is important for any child or teen is to be acknowledged. Both younger and older children need to see that their parent sees how hard they are working to ignore behavior and appreciates it. Just like children with DS, we all like to be noticed.

The above behavior was a pretty easy one to figure out and manage. After all, Morgan could ignore her brother's behavior and nothing terrible was going to happen. But what if it weren't so simple? What if Christopher was hitting her, breaking toys that she prized, or keeping her up at night by yelling or singing? Surely we cannot ignore such behaviors, right? Well, handling these types of behaviors are more complicated, but we can use some of the same principles. Perhaps this is a good time to stop and quiz yourself. What do YOU think we should do? Take a few moments and think about the principles you've learned and what you might do.

For these behaviors that are not so easy to ignore, we face a bit of a dilemma because the social and emotional reactions to them are still very reinforcing. Again, just like many other behaviors we have discussed, the yelling and crying Morgan does when Christopher bites her or throws her dolls out the window are pretty exciting for him. So, if Christopher is bored and he decides to become aggressive, that's a pretty good way to get some attention.

When behaviors such as this occur, we have to focus first on keeping everyone safe. If Morgan is being hit or otherwise injured, we need to make sure she can get away, and fast. And if her toys or other belongings are being broken or damaged, we need to secure them by locking her bedroom door or putting them in another safe place. We cannot let those behaviors keep going. As we will discuss in the chapter on discipline, when aggressive and negative behaviors occur, we have to be sure that anything fun goes away. If Christopher hits Morgan, she goes away. If he throws her toys out the window, he loses access to those toys.

But when Christopher does find a way to upset his sister, which is bound to happen, we also can manage her reaction. We can use the same strategies and help her stay calm, even with such upsetting behaviors. This will certainly be more difficult if he is actually hurting her. But I have worked with many siblings who can learn to change their reactions, especially when they understand why the behaviors are happening. For example, Morgan might be taught not to yell but to stay completely quiet, look away, and walk away as fast as possible to a room that Christopher cannot enter. He has just experienced "response-cost." In other words, if you hit your sister, she's gone.

While difficult to do, if Morgan can keep her emotions under control and simply go away, Christopher will learn very quickly that this is not a fun behavior. And that will make the behavior decrease. So, again, we are faced with some short-term pain for long-term gain. We need to help Morgan stay calm, and reward her like crazy for doing so, so that she will no longer reinforce her brother's behavior with her attention. We can add coins to her ignoring jar, praise her, and show acknowledgement in any way she appreciates. But the only way that behavior is going to improve is if we take away the *reaction*.

When brothers or sisters are very young, there are different challenges. For example, I worked with a five-year-old girl with DS who I will call Jamie. Jamie had a one-year-old baby brother, Omar, whom she loved to pieces. However, she also liked to push him over and hit him on the rear end. Naturally, their parents were horrified and scared. Unfortunately, we cannot ask a one-year-old to ignore such behaviors. It would not be safe, and it's also impossible. In this situation, I advised Jamie's parents to simply be vigilant. Anytime Jamie hit her brother, he was whisked away. The adults demonstrated how to interact with Omar nicely by cuddling him and playing peek-a-boo so that Jamie would have some options for good interactions. But whenever she whacked him, he was gone. While this was certainly a lot of work for her parents, it did get rid of that behavior. Jamie's parents removed the reinforcer (Omar), and the behavior was no longer fun. After all, what Jamie really wanted was to spend time with her brother. And she learned quickly that Omar had to be safe or that was not going to happen.

Chapter 7

Behavior Management in School and in the Community

The previous chapters outlined the basic steps in managing problem behaviors of children with DS at home. These same techniques can be used in many settings outside of the home, but of course, the stakes are higher because the repercussions can be more serious when behavior problems occur at school or out in the community. Your child may scare away potential friends, he may be excluded from certain activities, he may even endanger his life with unsafe behaviors—and of course, people may stare at you and your child.

The next section covers behavior management outside of the home. The ideas and solutions presented are just a small sample of the possibilities. As with the rest of this book, I hope that they help you understand these behaviors and how to respond to them. This way, when you face situations that aren't covered in the book, you can make your own educated guesses about what the underlying issues may be and come up with some good ideas about how to respond...*but don't react.*

Although having an exhaustive list of every problem you could face might sound appealing at first, I have found that parents and teachers do not have the time to read hundreds and hundreds of pages. After all, parenting and teaching are hard jobs! So, again, I encourage you to take these examples and think about the underlying lessons that can be applied to the individuals with Down syndrome in your life.

● ●

Behavior at School

We have discussed how to help siblings—maybe one or two children—ignore their brother's or sister's negative behaviors to help those behaviors go away. With only a couple of children, this is relatively easy. But what about a whole classroom of children? Who can imagine teaching dozens of students while ignoring and not reinforcing negative behaviors from one or more of the chil-

dren? For many children with DS, the classroom can remain a substantial trigger for negative behaviors even once their behaviors at home have been managed quite successfully. Classroom behavior management is daunting even for us "experts" in behavior management.

Fortunately, if you understand the basics of behavior, you can guess what strategies may be effective. If we see a negative behavior, we have to be careful not to reinforce it, or else that behavior will continue. So, in the classroom, teachers and other staff would ideally find some way to help the other children in the classroom not reinforce negative behaviors. They have to find some way to create structure, understanding, and, most challenging of all, *consistency* in ignoring negative behaviors.

So, how do we accomplish this? Well, the short answer is that we usually do not. In my experience, it is simply too challenging to negotiate the behavior of a large group of other children. One or two siblings we can handle, as discussed in the previous chapter. But twenty? This is beyond what I would consider taking on...but I would love to meet someone who would!

It is really important to point out what I am *not* suggesting. While we cannot require an entire classroom of children to ignore a classmate's negative behaviors, that does *not* mean that a child who is acting out should be sent to a separate space or the hallway to be isolated. Although separating a child who is acting out may be an immediate step, it is not a long-term solution.

Pinpointing What Leads to the Behavior

Rather than taking on such a herculean behavioral task as getting a room of kids to ignore inappropriate behavior, I choose to work around this issue. Instead, I work with the teachers and parents to identify and eliminate whatever is triggering or maintaining the behavior to begin with. I often talk with families and teachers about a few factors. First, when is the negative behavior happening? Is it during a specific period of the day, such as math? (Math is often the culprit, as it typically proves to be the most challenging subject for children with DS.) Does the behavior occur during transitions, another time of the day when things can be particularly difficult? We need information.

Luckily, in most school systems, there are behavioral experts on hand. Behaviorists in school are typically also skilled at analyzing behaviors and figuring out what is causing them. They collect lots of data and look closely at the "antecedents" (what comes before a behavior) and "consequences" (what happens after). This can help them to figure out what is driving a behavior. Often for children and teenagers with DS, the leading culprits are attention seeking and escaping or avoiding a disliked activity.

The formal way of assessing behavior issues in school is to request a functional behavior assessment, or *FBA*. The FBA involves having an expert in behavior, such as a board certified behavior analyst (BCBA) or psychologist, look at the triggers and reinforcers of behaviors. There is more information about FBAs later in this book, in chapter 12. At this point, however, you might be wondering if an FBA is a sort of punishment. After all, it sounds serious, and it's usually a bad sign when the school intervenes regarding behavior, right? Could this be the first step in removing a child from an inclusive setting? Well, this should not be, and is often not, the case. FBAs are very common. I think of them as a way of understanding behaviors, and most importantly, a way to prevent behaviors from interfering in your child's school experience.

The most important part of an FBA, in my opinion, is that it should lead to a positive behavior support plan, or *PBSP*. In other words, the goal of the FBA is to figure out why a behavior is occurring, and how to help a child do his or her best.

One very common example of school-based problems that I encounter is acting out during specific subjects or times of day. We need to look at what factors may be leading this to occur. Some children with situation-specific negative behaviors behave quite well throughout the school day. But when math (or another problematic subject) starts, they may run right out of the room, hit a classmate, or even strip all their clothes off right at their desk (yes, that is a true story). So, in a situation such as this, I often ask, "What's happening during math?"

Thinking Flexibly

This leads into a side discussion about my way of thinking about school in general. First, there is no perfect classroom for any child. As with any other aspect of life, there is always a trade-off in any given school setting. Perhaps inclusion time in a particular school is great, but the special education teacher in the learning center classroom is really amazing at teaching sight words, so you want your child to spend some time with her. But of course, if your child spends too much time in a specialized classroom, he is missing out on time with his typically developing peers.

Second, I believe that any time we are very set in our opinions (some would call this dogmatic), we can get ourselves into trouble. In other words, I try to always think flexibly and not get too stuck on an idea such as "this child must be included 100 percent of the time," or, conversely, "this child must be in a substantially separate classroom all day long!"

Let's use an example. Jonathan was a nine-year-old third grader. He had always been fully included and had done quite well socially, behaviorally, and academically. However, now that Jonathan was in third grade, he was finding math to be really hard. (Again, math was the culprit! Full disclosure: I love math and was a math tutor before graduate school. I promise this is not a vendetta against math!). So, every day around ten o'clock when math began, Jonathan started to be disruptive. He spat on classmates, ran out of the room, even tipped his desk over. Jonathan's teachers tried using time-out and supporting Jonathan's learning with visual aids. However, these techniques did not work. Rather, Jonathan often had to be escorted from the classroom and spend math time with a shared paraprofessional aide. The school was responding pretty reasonably, but nothing was working.

This led Jonathan's parents to ask for an appointment with me. As we discussed Jonathan's behavior in school, I learned that it was not occurring at home or at any other point of the school day.

I sometimes ask really simple questions. Scratch that, I *very often* ask simple questions. So, my question to Jonathan's parents was, "Should Jonathan be in the large classroom during math?"

This was, I knew, a loaded question. Jonathan had been 100 percent included up until third grade. I was taking a risk by even suggesting that, perhaps, this should change even in a very small way. And understandably, Jonathan's parents did react strongly to this question. Jonathan's parents told me that, from the time he had entered school, they had fought for inclusion. The school system had assumed he would and should be placed in a substantially separate classroom, and the family had had to "educate" the school administrators. And educate they did. After many letters and meetings, Jonathan had been placed in a typical preschool and had remained 100 percent included until this meeting with me. Jonathan seemed to have benefited a great deal from inclusion time: he had excellent social skills and language, and his academics were quite strong.

And now here I was, this "expert," suggesting that they throw away all this hard work? I would have been angry, too!

But here is the difference in our viewpoints—in my mind, inclusion is not all or nothing. It is not black or white. Inclusion, to me, means that an individual is meaningfully participating to the best of his ability in learning and in activities with peers. Now let's look at Jonathan's behavior at school again. While his IEP still stated that he was included for 100 percent of the school day (aside from speech and occupational therapies), was this really true? Was he truly "included" in math class, or was he just included on paper? When I discussed the reality with his parents, they again acknowledged that on most days, he was being "removed" from the classroom. They also felt the school had tried several reasonable approaches to manage this time of the day, but that they were not working.

I asked the family if they had ever considered adjusting his program so that he was included for most of the day—when it seemed to be benefiting him—but was given access to more individualized instruction for math. This had never crossed his parents' minds. They had fought so hard for "full inclusion" that the idea of ever letting that "full" part go seemed like a really bad idea.

So what happened? Well, after the parents had a few long conversations with me and another with the school, we decided on an experiment. The school agreed to place Jonathan in a math group with a special educator who would work with a maximum of three students, just for math, during the regular math period. Jonathan would remain included for the rest of the school day.

We also asked the school to start keeping track of what was happening. Rather than having teachers call the parents when things went wrong, we wanted to know when they were going right, and we wanted more information when they were going wrong. The school kept track of behavioral incidents all day long for one week before changing Jonathan's math program. Sure enough, almost all of his negative behaviors occurred during that period of the day. Then, we did a two-week experiment with Jonathan participating in the math group in a smaller classroom. He remained included for the rest of his school day. Lo and behold, we saw his behavior incidents drop down to near zero. Jonathan was not acting out and appeared happier in school throughout much of the day. He was also happier at home.

Perhaps you are saying to yourself, "Well, if you pull the child out of the classroom every time he acts out, perhaps he will behave better, but we just gave up his inclusion!" I think about this a bit differently. Recall that Jonathan was not really being included for math. Sure, his IEP said he was, but the reality was that he was being pulled out almost every day and spending that time with an aide, not learning math. And even worse, Jonathan's self-esteem was being affected and he was frustrated. After all, the school had to wait until he "failed" by acting out to remove him. So, Jonathan was basically waiting to fail each day and then being removed. Of course, it would have been ideal if the wonderful special education math teacher could have come into the larger classroom to teach Jonathan during math class. But in this school, that was not possible, at least not immediately. So, Jonathan was left with the two choices of being really unhappy in the inclusion setting, or receiving some math instruction in a smaller classroom.

Nobody wants to get into trouble at school. And when a child does, it usually means that something is not right. As I see it, because Jonathan was getting more of what he needed in math despite being outside of the general education classroom, he was actually more successfully included as a whole. His school day, overall, was more successful, he was feeling less frustrated, acting out far less, and feeling better about his school day. Jonathan was doing much better during other parts of his school day in the general classroom. If we think long term, which I *always* do, I have to imagine this will help Jonathan remain motivated for learning in the future as well. The less frustration and failure a child faces (and not that good character-building failure, but rather the "environment is not meeting my needs" type of failure), the better.

I have worked with many "Jonathans" and families like his over the years. And I have encountered this type of situation numerous times. It makes perfect sense to be cautious, or even scared, of giving up something so precious as full inclusion. It is something that families and clinicians like me fight for every day. But be careful not to be too rigid in your thinking. There is a lot of room between full inclusion and specialized classroom settings. And sometimes we have to make adjustments along that continuum to meet a child's needs in a particular school. And often, this can make the "big picture" a lot more successful for the student.

Developing a Clear Picture of the Problem Behavior

Surely, Jonathan's example is not the only sort of trouble that occurs in school. There are lots of reasons that a child or adolescent may avoid certain situations, subjects, or periods of the day. Perhaps he is being bullied at recess, is bothered by the noise in the crowded lunch room, or is struggling to adjust to a new music teacher. The big picture idea here is that we have to take a step back and try to determine what the problem is and then be flexible and creative in our attempts to solve it. The basic steps we need to take include:

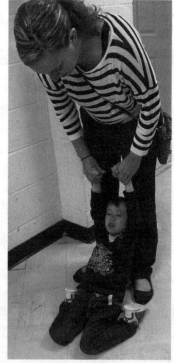

1. Describe the problem behavior.
2. Observe when it occurs and when it doesn't.
3. Make an educated guess about what is triggering the behavior and what is reinforcing it.
4. Create a *proactive* plan to prevent this behavior and provide the right supports.
5. Observe whether the plan worked.

And again, these steps should be undertaken with the support of the school, ideally through a formal functional behavior assessment (FBA), which is described in more detail in chapter 12.

Trouble with Transitions

In my experience, aside from difficulties with specific parts of the school day or particular subjects, the other most common behavioral challenge for children and teens with DS in school and in the community is difficulty with transitions. Again, it is challenging to control a larger environment, such as a classroom, completely. However, we can think about what problematic tasks such as transitioning involve and why they may be challenging. And this knowledge will help us know what may be helpful.

Families and teachers often tell me that transitioning—moving from one activity to another—is simply hard for children with DS. Why might this be? Well, think about some of those brain differences from earlier in this book. If processing new information is difficult, and hanging on to that information is even harder (if not presented in the right way), then something new or different may seem scary. And most people do not like the idea of doing something new or scary. We also learned about motivation differences. New tasks are hard. They require energy and effort. If someone's motivation is a bit lower than usual, particularly after a long day of working hard in school, then starting something new doesn't sound so fun. It is natural for the person to avoid it.

So, how can we deal with transition difficulties? Here are some behavioral "tricks of the trade" that can be very helpful for transitions and for managing other sorts of refusal in any setting, including at school or in the community.

First-Then

A common tool is the "First-Then" direction. I really like First-Then directions and routinely speak this way with children. First-Then is as simple as it sounds. First do x *(a task you don't want to do),* and then you can do/have/play y *(a task or item you do want).* Here are some examples for school:

- First line up, then recess.
- First reading, then dance party.
- First counting, then free time.
- First quiet work, then gym.

The possibilities are endless! Why does First-Then work so well? Well, First-Then accomplishes a lot of things. It helps with structure and predictability. We are telling the individual with DS what is going to happen, as well as the sequence of events. Knowing what will happen decreases anxiety, and less anxiety usually leads to better behavior and more cooperation (which is why Social Stories often work). But, in addition to providing structure and predictability, First-Then supports motivation. The adult is asking the child to do something but is building in a reward or preferred activity afterward. So, the child knows that something good is coming soon. When children are resisting something simple, such as a transition, I have found First-Then to be a really powerful tool.

And of course, using visuals for First-Then is even more helpful for many people with DS. Visual supports might be as simple as putting some Velcro strips on a piece of construction paper or poster board and sticking icons of various tasks as "first" or "then" items. However, many of us are lucky to also have a lot of technology at our fingertips these days. I have had a lot of good experiences with the "First-Then Visual Schedule" app, which is available on iTunes. This app allows you to create a First-Then visual schedule on the fly, or to make more advanced visual schedules and good behavior charts. The beauty of the app is that you can constantly change the schedule and have access to a huge selection of pictures without ever having to print anything.

Pairing Preferred and Nonpreferred Activities

Pairing preferred and nonpreferred activities is another simple technique that can help children with DS make transitions. When a child does not like to do something, we can often add something that he really likes to make that activity more appealing. For example, if a really sociable girl in a fifth-grade classroom refuses to line up for lunch, she might be assigned a line buddy. In other words, she could have a buddy with whom she could line up, and she could chat with her buddy to get ready for the transition. (For that matter, her classmates could have line buddies too.) All of a sudden, this dreaded change becomes not so dreadful; it becomes a time to see a friend. Some other examples include:

- Pair walking down the crowded, noisy hallway with special time with a best friend.
- Pair writing practice with listening to music.
- Pair playing with a squeeze ball with doing math problems.
- Pair a silent "dance party" with waiting for the bus to arrive.
- Pair reading practice with screen time using an educational website.

And here are some examples of using the pairing technique at home:

- Pair taking a bath with a favorite bath toy.
- Pair singing with potty time.
- Pair screen time with hair brushing.
- Pair swinging with practicing counting.

High P

High P refers to "high probability." This technique is built on the concept of "behavioral momentum." In other words, once an individual is headed down a behavioral path, such as breaking all the rules or following all the rules, he can build up a sort of "head of steam" and keep going down that path.

I have worked with many children with Down syndrome who are in a bad pattern with a parent or a teacher and are getting lots of negative feedback. All of a sudden, even the things they used to like to do become a challenge, and they respond to them with a "NO!" or a flop to the floor. High P techniques involve changing that momentum in a short period of time by asking the child to engage in many behaviors that are likely to be successful and then providing him with lots of praise. For example, at home you might say, "Give me a high five! Now jump up and down! Now let's sing our favorite song! And now let's put our dishes in the sink!" Had you started with a request to put the dishes in the sink, your child might have refused. You might have even seen a stop and flop. But if you can have some fun by starting with some high probability requests and build up some positive momentum, you may suddenly find that your child is doing exactly as you asked, and happily so!

Similarly, at homework time, you can start by having your child work on less demanding tasks such as a worksheet with counting and simple addition problems before going on to the harder, new problems that he is working on in class. Nobody likes to get things "wrong," and this is very true for individuals with DS. So, if you can start with some success, you may help your child put in better effort for the more challenging work ahead.

And of course, this strategy can be used in school and in the community. Let's take the example of Erica, a fifteen-year-old girl with DS who is refusing to complete her science classwork. Based on what you have read so far and your own experiences, you probably know that if Erica's one-to-one aide threatens her with a time-out or punishment of some sort, she is not likely to respond well. Still, Erica is simply sitting at her desk and refusing to work, and the struggle to get her to work is disrupting the classroom. What if Erica's aide, John, tried to use High P? He could start by thinking of things that Erica likes to do, such as write poems and talk about her favorite singer. John might begin by asking Erica to write down one of her favorite poems and then tell her how great it is. Then, he might ask her some questions about her favorite singer, Lady Gaga. Again, John should show genuine interest and enthusiasm for the topic (hopefully he doesn't dislike Lady Gaga too much!).

After changing the "momentum" of Erica's behavior, John might again try prompting Erica to focus on her science assignment. He may even throw in a First-Then, such as "First science work, then let's play a Lady Gaga video!" In this situation, John has changed the direction of Erica's behavior from negative to positive and has built up some momentum that may help Erica complete her work.

Acting Out in Community Settings

Another common behavior problem for families of all children, and especially for families of children with DS, is acting out in public. I cannot count how many families have complained about their children's disruptive behaviors in grocery stores, malls, or other public settings. I should start with an admission—I also hate the grocery store! If we think about what the grocery store entails, it is not particularly fun, it is usually crowded and loud, and there's not much to do aside from finding food. Similarly, many families have told me about challenges in parking lots and going from one place to another. We have already discussed that children with DS often do not like transitions and that change can be particularly challenging. So this is not a surprising behavior problem if we understand how the brain works for people with Down syndrome. But of course, understanding the problem is only half the battle.

To address problem behaviors in public, we have to keep in mind the same ideas and strategies we have discussed throughout this book. We have to remember that our own reactions, and giving attention to behaviors, can be very counterproductive. If we become upset and animated, this can be very reinforcing of a behavior. Remember, when adults become upset, it's very exciting to children with DS on a brain-based level, and that makes the behavior more likely to occur.

Basic Steps in Responding to Behavior in the Community

The first step in responding to behavior problems in public is to make sure you do not make this behavior fun or interesting. For instance, if your child is pulling items off the shelf and dropping them on the floor in the grocery store, do *not* do any of the following:

- Make eye contact.
- Speak loudly.
- Show strong emotions in your facial expressions.

You may be saying to yourself as you read this, "Uh oh!" Not to worry—we all have these reactions. But the purpose of this book is to teach you to be thoughtful about your reactions so you can help your child with DS behave at his or her best.

For negative behaviors in public, you often do have to respond and take action. However, you do not have to do so emotionally. You do not have to look at your child and yell, and you do not need to show strong emotions on your face. It is challenging *not* to do this, but with a little practice, you can. I have worked with many families who have gotten the hang of this and have seen incredible improvement in their child's behavior.

The second step in responding to a child's behavior in public is to think about the function of the behavior. Why is this behavior occurring where it is occurring? For instance, if it happens in the grocery store, think about the *structure* of a grocery trip, and you will start to see some reasons why your child might act out. Consider the following:

- The grocery store is boring, and there is not much for a child to do.
- Trips to the grocery store are long, and it's hard to know when they will end.
- There is temptation everywhere. If you're bored, those cheese curls look especially good and fun! (Another confession…I love cheese curls!)

After thinking about what the grocery store is like for children with DS, it becomes a little clearer why they may act out in this setting. So, how can we address these issues and make the grocery store a friendlier place for children with DS? Stop for a moment and try to guess what our strategies might be. As usual, think about the brain and what strengths and weaknesses this group of people usually has. What might work?

Well, to start, I like to add structure and make the visit to the grocery store an opportunity for learning and positive behavior.

How can we turn a visit to such a hectic place as a grocery store into a rewarding learning experience for a child? Make a grocery list, of course! For a child with DS, the list should be relatively brief, include lots of visuals (or all visuals), and be genuinely helpful to the family. If the child can actually be helpful, Dad will be happy, the child will sense that, and everyone will receive benefits from the interaction.

A young child may need to sit in the cart with a list and will often need a lot of help to get through the visit. A school-age child with DS would be expected to stay with his mom or dad, carry his list, and look for the items he needs. Of course, he may need help finding them or picking the right brand. As the child moves into adolescence, he may be able to shop independently (and what a good skill to develop!) and meet his mom or dad after a few minutes of looking for items alone. As a parent, you can estimate better than I can what your child is capable of doing in the community. And to start, I suggest trying to use a list when you are on a shorter grocery trip, ideally at a quieter time of day.

The idea is to start small and build up to longer, more hectic trips. The purpose here, however, is adding structure, visuals, and positive reinforcement to a difficult situation. The above example of a grocery trip is just one example of how we can deal with a very common challenge for families. Below, I provide a guide for how to structure grocery shopping and other community outings.

But before we get to the specifics of how you can approach community outings, let's look at what our changes to the grocery trip do for a child or adolescent with DS. All of a sudden, grocery shopping is not a never-ending, boring trip with no fun at all. Instead, it is a time when the child can go on a scavenger hunt, find items on his own (which is learning a new skill, most likely), and be genuinely helpful to a parent. And being genuinely helpful has huge rewards—children can see how much they are appreciated by their dad or mom, and that makes them feel great. On top of that, they now have some sense of when this whole thing will be over. (Ideally, I like the child's shopping list to include some items throughout the store so that all along the way, there will be items to find. And when

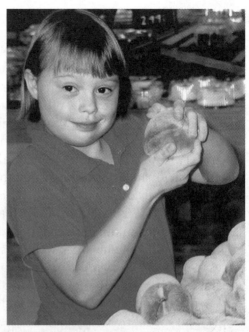

the child is reaching the end of the list, he knows that his trip is almost over).

You are not going to be surprised to learn that you should probably provide a reward, or "motivator," for the end of the grocery trip. After all, mustering the motivation for less interesting tasks can be a challenge for children with DS. You can likely provide some motivation all along by asking for your child's help picking out groceries. However, if you can add a prize at the end for a job well done, he will likely do even better. In addition, if you have any trouble with your child along the way, you can remind him of the prize, perhaps by showing a First-Then visual schedule like the ones you can make on the First-Then Visual Schedule App (available from Apple's App Store), and help get things back on track. This is, of course, a better choice than responding by yelling or becoming upset in the store. (See the next section for an example of using this technique to keep a child on track if he likes to stop and flop.)

Dealing with "Stop and Flop" Behavior

Let's use an example to illustrate how you might reduce stopping and flopping by building some rewards for your child into a community outing.

I recently saw a seven-year-old girl with Down syndrome whom I will refer to as Luz. Luz does not become aggressive or have behaviors that get her into big trouble. However, when her parents take her out, she can become tired, irritable, and frustrated. She often stops and flops in stores, usually in the middle of a busy aisle, and refuses to budge. Of course, her parents have been frustrated, and at times, embarrassed. They often raise their voices, become animated, and try to convince her to move with promises of a reward or threats of losing her iPad. Does this sound familiar? All the promises and threats have not worked, however, because the underlying problem—that Luz is overwhelmed, bored, and frustrated—is not being addressed.

Luz's parents came to my office at their wit's end, wanting to talk about how to punish Luz. It was only natural that punishment was on their minds, as Luz was causing a lot of disruption to the family and to total strangers in the grocery store. The family was naturally frustrated. But as a budding expert in behavior and DS, you know that there are many strategies to consider and try that have nothing to do with punishment.

I talked with Luz's family about making her a visual schedule with a shopping list and building in some rewards. We chose a few items for her list (about three to five items work well for school-age children) from different places in the store. I advised them to keep the trip short. The goal at the start was not to get through the entire family shopping list. Instead, it was to help Luz learn to tolerate the grocery store and a busy community setting with her family. This meant that Luz would walk through the store with her parents, and every five or ten minutes, she would get to find an item on her list (do something fun) and be praised by her family.

I also talked with Luz and her family about her favorite activities, such as playing on her iPad, playing outside with her brother, and dancing to music. We decided, with Luz's help, that dancing to music would be a great reward for finding all of her items. This is an important point—we did *not* decide to reward her for "not acting out" or "being a good girl" in the grocery store. No, we planned to reward her for doing something positive—finding the items on her list—calling attention only to the good stuff, not the bad stuff.

Here is a sample of Luz's shopping list and reward:

As you can see, this grocery list with a reward at the end is nothing fancy at all. It took me about five minutes to make on the computer, for free, using programs that I already own. The amazing thing is that this little tool that took five minutes to make completely changed Luz's behavior in the grocery store. She was very excited to go and then was very excited to find each of her items. Notably, Luz did not mind when her father asked her to grab a different item, such as a different brand, than the one she picked first. Luz was happy to trade for one as long as her father acknowledged that it was "her job" to do it. Her father was thrilled when she found the items. He praised her with a "Great job, Luz!" and also showed with his facial expression that he was genuinely proud of her and that she was helping. And at the end of the trip, her father was thrilled to play some music and dance around the house with her. It was a great trip for all involved.

Over time, Luz's grocery trips gradually became longer and longer until she could tolerate a full grocery trip. But remember, slow and steady wins the race; we have to build up to long outings slowly and with a lot of success and encouragement along the way.

The example above illustrates the successful use of behavioral momentum to change behavior for the better. Consider what was happening before Luz had her grocery list. She had no structure, grocery trips seemed to take *forever*, and she had nothing to do. Acting out was really one of her only options. And naturally, her father became very frustrated. Luz then processed that frustration with her social-emotional radar, and she felt bad. Nobody likes disappointing someone they care about. When we feel bad, we become cranky. When we are cranky, we are less motivated. So, is it really a surprise that Luz used to take items from the shelves and throw them or sit down in the middle of the aisle? Both the momentum of her behavior and the interaction with her father were very negative.

Once we implemented a grocery list for Luz, the momentum changed completely. All of a sudden, she was excited to be in the store. She had a job to do, after all! And her father was very happy that she was helping and not acting out. Luz felt great when she made her father happy. And she naturally wanted to keep doing well. Now the momentum was very positive and powerful.

Guide to a Successful Community Outing

Of course, grocery stores are certainly not the only place where families go or where people with DS can act out. However, they are the place that I hear about the most from families. Let's go through the basic steps in having successful outings so that you can follow them for yourself when you are venturing out:

1. ***Start small.*** Go for a shorter time, when things are less hectic, to start building the skills. Make sure your child is not too tired or hungry.

2. *Make a plan.* What do you want to occur? Make a plan and show it to your child or adolescent in the form of a visual schedule or a Social Story.

3. *Add structure.* What can the child or adolescent do during this outing? What could his goal be? When shopping, a shopping list is helpful. When going to the doctor, consider bringing along a word search, homework from a favorite class, or an educational game that he can play.

4. *Add a reward.* What can the child earn if the trip is successful? Some special time with you, the adult? Screen time? Choosing a place to eat lunch afterward?

5. *Get excited!* Remember, the emotional response an individual with DS receives can be more powerful than any other reward. So, when things go well in community outings, show how excited you are! Heap on that praise; be enthusiastic. Your enthusiasm will only help with the next time.

6. *Go forward slowly.* After you have some success in the community, go slowly. It is tempting to say, "I fixed it!" and then go right to a marathon grocery trip on Sunday evening when the store is crowded. Don't fall into that trap. Instead, go to the store or out in the community for just a little bit longer, with just a slightly longer list. Build up slowly to keep that success going.

Dealing with Bolting

Another problematic behavior that often occurs in public is bolting. For example, the family or class has taken a trip into the city, and the child with DS runs off. Most often, particularly with young children, this behavior is accompanied by a smile. Families often describe to me, usually with a traumatized look in their eyes, how their child ran off in a dangerous setting such as a parking lot or a busy street and looked back, waiting to be chased, smiling at the family as if this was a game.

This behavior is incredibly stressful for any family. Bolting reaches a new level of problem behavior because someone could get hurt. It is natural and only human to become very upset about this behavior.

Let's think about why this behavior occurs so frequently in children with Down syndrome. First, we know that impulse control, or taking a moment to think about what a behavior will lead to, can be hard for individuals with DS. I often think about this as "not seeing the stop signs." Often, if they get upset with a sibling or classmate or see something interesting across the street, they don't stop and think, "Hmm, how should I respond to this?" Instead, individuals with DS are prone to simply act without considering the consequences.

We also know that those with DS are typically very socially engaged and love getting reactions from other people. Again, that social-emotional radar is very powerful. So, very often, children with DS learn quickly that running away from a parent or teacher gets a really big emotional reaction. In other words, on a very basic brain-based level, it's fun!

If you think about these aspects of how people with DS learn and see the world, it is not surprising that bolting can be a real problem. So, how should you respond?

What Not to Do

For many children, bolting becomes an attention-seeking behavior. When you get upset, make lots of eye contact, raise your voice, and make strong facial expressions, your child is likely to experience your reaction as fun. It is very hard for us as adults to understand because we are, quite obviously, *not having fun*! But again, for people with DS who are highly attuned to other people, this is like winning a slot machine game—all the lights are flashing and it's entertaining! Furthermore, lecturing your child about not running off is not likely to help, nor is telling him about all the horrible things that could happen. Remember, all that language is not doing much good, and your child is instead probably processing more of your emotion (which can be fun!) rather than getting the message you want to send.

What to Do

When Your Child Is Running Away: Here are a few things to keep in mind. First, you have to keep everyone safe. So, go and get that child and do not let him run into the street! That is, of course, most important. Second, if you want this behavior to stop, you have to be sure to keep your reactions in check. This, again, is where the strategy of respond...*but don't react* comes into play. Run after the child and keep him safe, but do so without becoming upset, making eye contact, or yelling, all of which may seem fun and interesting, and keep the behavior going.

Oftentimes, I have to show families what I mean at this point. Picture a child running off in a parking lot. Of course, this is completely terrifying. You *must* go get that child to keep him safe. But aside from grabbing the child to keep him safe, are any other reactions necessary? What good are they doing? They *feel good* to us as adults, because we are terrified and we want to express that fear. But these reactions can be completely counterproductive in terms of behavior management over the long term. Instead of expressing to a child how important it is that he not do this ever again, the words coming out of our mouths may be meaningless, and we have instead taught the child that this is a very effective way to get *lots* of attention. So, again, I suggest that you respond...*but don't react.*

You may be asking yourself at this point, "Is this guy telling me to go grab my child after he ran off in the parking lot and just stay quiet?" Well, not exactly. You do need to respond, but you also need to stay calm so that you don't send a message that this is a fun behavior. And you also need to consider why this behavior is happening. Is it an impulse control issue? Is your child bored so when he sees something interesting, he decides to go get it? Are there strategies in place to prevent this from happening in the first place?

The answers to these questions may be complicated, and may also change from situation to situation. However, the strategies to help with bolting are pretty consistent across situations. As discussed above, everybody must keep their reactions in check. This applies to parents, teachers, and, to the extent possible, other children such as peers and siblings.

When a child bolts, go get that child, remain calm, and do not make eye contact or use a lot of words. Instead, hold the child's hand or arm, get him to safety, and gently state, "No running." Honestly, it is very difficult to remain calm when your child's safety is at risk. But this is the only way to make bolting less fun and interesting and decrease the behavior so it happens less frequently, if at all.

Before Your Child Runs Away: The best strategy, as usual, is to prevent the behavior from happening in the first place. Of course, safety is the most important thing to consider. So, I do not suggest locking children in their rooms or doing anything else that could create a fire hazard. The following strategies, however, may be helpful in the home:

- Place locks on the front and back doors of the house that only the adults can reach.
- Install alarms on doors and windows that will go off if your child tries to leave without you.
- Create visual supports such as stop signs and place them on the doors to remind your child that he is not supposed to go outside on his own.

- Invest in a GPS system. GPS systems can be incredibly helpful and safe. GPS systems have come a long way, and children can wear bracelets or even orthotics in their shoes with tracking devices in them.
- Contact the local police department and neighbors. Chat with them about your child's or adolescent's needs so that they have a heads-up if they ever need to become involved.

This type of planning can make dealing with bolting incidents much smoother and less stressful down the road. And as children age, this is one behavior that does often go away as impulse control improves.

Preventing bolting in public is, of course, more complicated. Still, some of the same ideas apply. The first step is to review any structures and safeguards that may already be in place. Does the child know the rules for walking in public? Are there any rules? One rule that I often recommend is for families to teach their children to hold hands or do another behavior that is incompatible with running. Some families may be able to teach this rule by practicing holding hands in public during a "low stakes" scenario. You could also use a Social Story to teach your child that he needs to hold hands when walking in public. Of course, you can apply this rule in your own way. Perhaps your child prefers to hold on to mom's purse (that she is carrying) rather than her hand. Any option that is incompatible with running is fair game. Other

children and some adolescents need to remain in a stroller to stay safe in public. Again, the first priority is for everyone to remain safe.

Another strategy to use in addition to holding hands is to build in a structure around these difficult times. Specifically, if your child tends to run off in public, you can add in some motivation for your child to stay with the family. As usual, an example is helpful:

Jaden and his family belong to the YMCA, which is located in a large shopping center. Jaden loves the YMCA and his swim class in particular. However, when the family arrives and opens the car door, Jaden sometimes runs off into the parking lot without an adult. Jaden laughs and laughs, looking back at his family to see who will chase him. Despite his family being very upset and yelling for him to come back, he thinks this is great fun.

When I met with Jaden's family, we discussed their attempts to use time-out, yelling, taking away screen time, and several other punishments to manage this behavior. Not surprisingly, those strategies did not work. Jaden seemed to become so excited in the moment that he was not really considering the consequences of running off, only that it was fun right at that time.

I spent some time getting to know Jaden and his family. It turns out that he loves playing a reading game on his iPad, and he is relatively responsible with the iPad. Jaden also is a very visual learner. He responds very well to visual schedules in school, and his school uses video modeling (see the box below) to help him learn new skills.

What Is Video Modeling?

Video modeling is very much like it sounds. It involves making videos of individuals completing tasks or engaging in an activity to teach a child, teen, or adult skills and positive behaviors. Often, video modeling is most effective when the video is taken of that same individual completing the task or activity to the best of his ability. Just as with Social Stories, the idea is to show the *desired* behaviors so the individual learns what is expected. Children with Down syndrome tend to respond very well to video modeling since it uses the visual strengths of the individual to *show* him, rather than *tell* him, what we would like him to do. For more information about video modeling, please see: http://www.watchmelearn.com/video-modeling/what-is-video-modeling.

For Jaden, we combined a couple techniques to work on his bolting. First, his brother, Sam, volunteered to be filmed walking from the car to the YMCA. He held his mother's hand the entire time. Next the video showed Sam entering the YMCA, where his mother handed him the iPad and let him play Jaden's favorite educational game. We set up a timer so that the game would only last five minutes. Jaden viewed the video of his brother several times and then his parents caught him on a good day and made the same video with him. Again, Jaden watched the video several times. In the meantime, Jaden's mother also practiced keeping her cool.

The next time Jaden went to the YMCA and his mother parked the car, he immediately grabbed her hand and said, "iPad, Mommy!" He now knew the rules and what was expected of him. And he wanted to earn his game. His mother held Jaden's hand, and he got out of the car. Immediately, Jaden started to pull away from his mother. Rather than yelling or losing her cool, however, Jaden's mother stayed calm, held his hand, and said gently, "First walk, then iPad." Jaden stopped pulling, and shortly he was safely in the YMCA, happily playing his game.

If you recall the discussion on behavioral momentum, you might expect that once Jaden successfully made this transition from the car to the parking lot a few times, he would be more likely to comply. And this was, in fact, the case. He did very well from then on. The family then took these ideas and applied them to other situations. They always held Jaden's hand for transitions and always built in a motivator at the end. While Jaden would still try to pull away at times, his parents were now holding his hand (and usually holding tight!), so he couldn't get away so easily. His new rules were incompatible with running. If he tried to pull his hand away and run, his parents could just remind him gently about his reward to get him back on track. And the entire time, they did not get overly emotional. This, of course, helped their relationship and lowered the stress in their family. They had learned to use the "respond, but don't react" method.

The next chapter covers additional techniques for handling bolting and other problem behaviors when prevention does not work.

Chapter 8

Discipline

Whenever I speak about behavior publically or with families, people are curious about discipline. And by *discipline* they usually mean punishment for inappropriate behavior.

If you've read the previous chapters, you know there are many techniques that can be effective for preventing negative behaviors and encouraging positive behaviors for individuals with Down syndrome. And when those techniques are effective, discipline doesn't even have to enter the picture.

Now, this is not just me being a "softie" as a pediatric psychologist. For all children, these positive and preventative strategies, often called "positive behavior supports," simply work better than discipline. In fact, the special education laws in the United States require that school staff try using positive behavior supports (PBS) to manage behavior challenges before they use punishment, because the research on the effectiveness of PBS is so clear. In my opinion, this is even more true for individuals with DS. Why is that?

Think back to a time when you, as a parent, teacher, or other professional, disciplined a child. We can assume that the child broke a pretty significant rule or was really testing your patience. Now try to remember how you were feeling at the time. Were you happy, excited, anxious, angry? Most often, adults are emotional when we discipline. Usually, a child has done something that scared us, frustrated us, or brought about some other strong feelings. We usually do not discipline in an emotionally neutral way. So, when we are upset and disciplining, we are very likely to do the things that adults do when they are angry:

- Make lots of eye contact.
- Raise our voice.

- Make strong facial expressions.
- Use a lot of words.

As we have learned, each of these reactions can actually be very reinforcing. They make behaviors worse, not better. While this is likely true for most children, it is particularly true for those with DS. Remember, people with DS have highly tuned social-emotional radar.

Effective Disciplinary Techniques

Even though it's almost always better and more effective to prevent a child's problem behaviors than to punish her for them, sometimes children with DS need discipline. Of course, discipline is not the final word. I encourage you to use these strategies for only a very short time while you figure out why the behavior is happening and learn to prevent it. But when you do need to respond to a behavior after it has occurred, remember that there are effective and ineffective ways to do it. When choosing a disciplinary strategy for children with DS, you have to be thoughtful and not rely on your gut adult instincts to discipline.

Withholding Attention: Planned Ignoring

As discussed throughout the book, our emotional reactions often play a big role in maintaining behavior problems in children and teenagers with Down syndrome. So, not surprisingly, if we withhold our emotional reactions, that can be a very powerful form of discipline for negative behaviors. In other words, if we want a behavior to stop, we can try taking our strong reactions and emotions away.

Let's use an example to illustrate the point. Lucas is a five-year-old boy with DS who often pinches his parents and his older sister. When he does so, his family members tend to yelp in pain, look directly at him, and often yell something like, "Lucas, no pinching—that really hurts!" And of course, Lucas then laughs and giggles, celebrating the reaction that he was looking for the whole time. Clearly, Lucas is looking for attention. And what is also quite clear is that he is getting it!

This behavior has gone on for months, and the family is at the end of their rope. They have tried time-outs, raising their voices, and taking away Lucas's favorite toys when he pinches. And nothing seems to work. When I met with Lucas's family, I suggested that when he pinches, the family member look away from him, say nothing, and remain emotionally neutral. I suggested that they block his pinching to protect themselves but not respond to him in any way. They could even walk away. The family left my office feeling quite skeptical about this "punishment" of basically doing nothing. However, a week later, the family returned and said they felt they had witnessed a miracle. Lucas stopped pinching almost completely after only a couple of days once his family stopped reacting so strongly to it. Beyond that, he hated being ignored so much that he quickly began to look at his sister and his parents in a way that seemed to say, "What can I do to get your attention!?"

His family was astonished at how much power there was in just their eye contact, their facial expressions, and their tones of voice. They were amazed that just not responding could have such an impact on Lucas's behavior. We then discussed Lucas's desire for attention and came up with many positive things he could do to earn some. We created a chore chart, as discussed in chapter 5, and settled on a few jobs that Lucas could do, such as filling the dog's water bowl. When he wanted attention, instead of pinching, which would no longer be effective, Lucas could now do some jobs around the house that his family would genuinely appreciate. And of course, when he did his jobs, his family praised him and commented on how helpful he was. Once this plan was implemented, he sensed that appreciation and very quickly started to develop some positive behavioral momentum.

So, the first step in effective discipline for those with DS is again to be aware of our own reactions. Our responses can be great motivators, and we should react strongly when we observe good behavior that we want to see continue. But we can also have a profound impact by taking our reactions away when we want a behavior to stop.

This brings us back to the basics of behavior management. If we want a behavior to continue, we usually want to *add something* such as a motivator or reward. If we want a behavior to stop, we usually want to *take something away*. This is the underlying principle behind time-out. In a time-out, we remove fun or exciting activities or objects to ensure we do not reinforce the behavior. We are taking all the reinforcers away. For many individuals with DS, the biggest reinforcer is *other people*. So, we can take ourselves and our emotional and social reactions away. This is the most important thing to know about discipline for individuals with DS. Removing other people and their reactions can be the most powerful "punishment" of all.

This disciplinary technique is called *planned ignoring*. This term highlights the fact that we aren't just ignoring a child altogether. Rather, we are intentionally and planfully ignoring certain behaviors. And we are intentionally and planfully *not ignoring* other behaviors (e.g., good ones!).

Planned ignoring is another strategy that families and teachers can often have trouble buying into. Who is this guy telling us to just *ignore* everything? That sounds like something a psychologist would say! It sure does. But just like many other seemingly simple concepts that we have covered so far in this book, it's not so simple. Ignoring can be really hard and really complicated. And families almost always point out—you cannot ignore everything!

Determining Which Behaviors to Ignore

In my opinion, the best approach to determining what behaviors should be ignored and what should not comes from Ross Greene, a psychologist who was on the Harvard faculty for many years. Dr. Greene's model is called Collaborative and Proactive Solutions (CPS) and is a really ingenious and comprehensive way to think about behavior in all children. He has been quite successful in improving behavior in very tough environments, including inpatient psychiatric units and camps for children with behavior issues.

Dr. Greene originally explained his model in a book called *The Explosive Child* (see Suggested Reading at the back of the book). One of the highlights of the book is Dr. Greene's explanation of how to determine which behaviors are worth responding to and which are not. This is just a small piece of his work, but it is very helpful when we are trying to figure out what we should and should not ignore. Dr. Greene currently breaks down responding to behaviors in three "steps." Please note that the below is my own interpretation of Dr. Greene's model, not a word-for-word or by any means complete description of his work. But here's how I think about it:

- *Step 1:* This step includes behaviors that are unsafe, to which we have to respond. For example, running into the street or hitting a sibling.
- *Step 2:* This step includes behaviors that are not unsafe but may or may not be a high priority for a family. This is where most behavioral work can be done and lessons can be learned. A family has to decide whether a Step 2 behavior is worth dealing with at any time. I usually tell families to think about whether a behavior is currently in the top three issues they want to address. If it is not, we wait. If it is a major priority, we get to work. Examples of this type of behavior include using swear words or refusing to eat at the dinner table.
- *Step 3*: This is a very important step for families and teachers of children with DS to understand how to address. This step is made up of the *annoying* behaviors that are not really causing

any harm. Some examples include refusing to wear a certain color shirt, chewing with the mouth open, and humming.

Categorizing behaviors in this manner is very helpful because it lets us organize our thinking so we can plan out a response. And if we can plan out how we will manage a behavior based on a good understanding of it, we are way ahead of the game.

The other really helpful aspect of using the step approach is that it is, in itself, an intervention. I have worked with many families who have been bothered by one or more behaviors that are really just annoying but not doing any harm. Again, these might include humming, tongue clicking, or making other silly noises. After learning about the steps, many families return to my office and say, "We decided that was a Step 3." The truly remarkable thing is that when families start to ignore these behaviors, many of them go away! If the behavior does not go away, there may be another reason for it, such as stimming to relax. See chapters 4 and 9 for insights on dealing with those types of behaviors.

For now, suffice it to say that there are likely at least a few behaviors that you are bothered by that may require no intervention at all. They just require "tuning out" or planned ignoring. And because most individuals with DS are quite social, getting rid of your own reactions to the behavior may be enough to make it go away.

Handling Step 2 Behaviors

For behaviors that fall into Step 2, we also have some relatively simple options. Remember, behavior is driven by incentives or *motivators*. So, if you want a behavior to happen again, you should respond to it and add motivators to the situation. If you want a behavior to stop, you need to remove incentives and motivators. When you see a behavior that is not a safety issue but is among your top three concerns, you need to think about what can be taken away. Here are some things that can be taken away and some examples of removing them in specific situations:

Remove the Child

In some situations, such as a birthday party in which a child is being disruptive or aggressive, there is a simple option. You can leave the birthday party. This is most effective for young children whose parents can easily move them from one place to another pretty easily. Here's an example:

James is a five-year-old boy with Down syndrome who is having a great time at a classmate's birthday party. He has been having fun bowling, eating pizza, and dancing to music. However, after a couple of hours, he is looking tired and has started to become sillier. James has pinched a couple of other kids and is making silly noises that his friends do not like. His parents begin by giving him a time-out, asking him to sit in a chair away from the group. This does not last long, however, and James quickly runs back to the group, where he engages in the same behaviors. So, James's parents remove him from the party and take him home. They tell him it is time to go and state, "First car, then iPad." James happily goes out to the car, and the family drives home.

You may ask yourself, should James's parents let him get away with no punishment? Shouldn't he learn that what he did was wrong? Well, ideally, yes, he should learn that. However, do you think that at James's age and developmental level, he is going to learn that lesson? Further, do you think that a time-out or other punishment is going to teach it? And finally, what do you think is causing this behavior? Does James just feel like driving his friends bonkers, or is he tired and sending his parents a message that he needs to leave?

By now you know that I believe that children do not act out just to bother other people. Rather, their behavior is a way of communicating. James was telling his parents, "I'm done!" and they needed to turn off their adult gut reactions—to say that he was "being bad"—and try to figure out what he needed. In this case, what he needed was to leave. And remember, this *is,* in itself, an intervention and really a punishment. After all, threatening to take away screen time or dessert later in the day probably won't have much of an effect on his behavior right then. But removing James right then and there was probably 1) what he needed, and 2) the best way to teach that this behavior was not okay.

Remove Others

Sometimes removing a child or teenager is not a good option. Some children become aggressive or refuse to move, and in some situations we do not have a good place for them to go. In these cases, the next step is to think about what else can be removed from the situation. Remember, the first option is to remove others' reactions. So, a parent or teacher can remove eye contact, language, and emotion, and this is often very effective for individuals with DS.

But what if other children are present? In a small group, we may choose to ask those children to leave the area. We are, most likely, removing one of the big reinforcers or motivators for the behavior. When children are acting out and being aggressive, this may be the best option. Similarly, I have worked with many children who are aggressive to pets. In those situations, time-outs, yelling, and other typical forms of discipline do not work very well.

What often does work is taking away the pet, at least temporarily. Here is an example of using this strategy:

Tim is a ten-year-old boy with Down syndrome, and his family recently got a puppy. Tim loves the puppy but can be impulsive and is having a hard time being gentle with the dog. He can play rough and has even hit the dog a number of times. His parents tried time-out, scolding, and taking away his computer time, with no effect.

When I met with Tim's family, we decided that whenever Tim was aggressive toward the dog, they should take away the biggest motivator—the dog! So, Tim's family began letting him play with the dog only with a parent watching. If he was aggressive to the dog in any way, his parents said calmly but clearly, "No hit," and took the dog to another part of the house where Tim was not allowed to join him. To show Tim what they did want him to do, his parents demonstrated how to rub the dog's belly. And when he did that without being aggressive, they praised him like crazy! Before long, Tim learned that if he hit the dog, the dog went away, but if he rubbed the dog's belly, everyone was happier.

So, again, when you are responding to a behavior after it has occurred, you want to remove rewarding things rather than add them. And to review, this can include taking away your reactions (the most powerful thing you can do), taking away a child, or taking away other motivators (e.g., other children, pets, etc.). Time-out is based on this idea. And time-out can be a good technique for discipline, including for individuals with Down syndrome.

Time-Out

You must be careful when using time-out. You cannot be angry, or at least you cannot show it, when you give a time-out. You have to keep your tone of voice neutral, limit eye contact, and keep your facial expressions in check. As I have emphasized, having strong reactions, even when disciplining, can actually make a behavior worse. In addition, I have worked with many children who have come to think of time-out as a big deal and a very unpleasant thing. In other words, the child has strong emotions tied to the concept or to the words "time-out," which is not good when you are trying to work on behavior. As a result, I often like to use other terms besides *time-out*. I often like to say, "Take a break" or "Take a rest." These terms are less emotionally charged, and they do not send the message, "You are in trouble; you are bad!" That can be a very difficult message for children with Down syndrome to accept, given their strong social-emotional radars.

Another very important consideration when using time-outs or other forms of discipline is to determine whether the child understands what is happening. If your goal is to teach a lesson and prevent a behavior from re-

curring, you have to be sure that the child gets the message. I often ask that a child explain her discipline to me. If she can say, demonstrate, sign, or use a device to tell me how a consequence is linked to her behavior, then I say, go ahead with the time-out (or "take a break"). For example, she might tell me, "If I pinch my brother, I get a time-out." But, if a child does not appear to really understand the punishment and the connection between her behavior and the consequence, you aren't really likely to be teaching much. For this reason, I do not often recommend these types of discipline strategies. I much prefer to figure out why a behavior is happening and prevent it or respond to a behavior by removing reactions, the child herself, or others. It just plain works better, most of the time.

Handling Step 1 Behaviors

Perhaps the most troubling part of behavior management for many families is figuring out how to handle those really scary, unsafe behaviors that fall into the Step 1 category. You cannot ignore those behaviors, and you do not have a lot of time to think of creative solutions when safety is at risk. You have to *respond*. But remember, while you must respond to unsafe behaviors, you do not need to *react* to them. Remember, it is your reactions—the loud voice, the intense eye contact, and the strong facial expressions—that can make bad behavior so much fun for children. It is not that the adults are responding; it is that they are going a little bonkers! And let's be honest, didn't you find it just a tiny bit fun to drive adults a little nuts as a kid? I know I did.

Perhaps the best example of a Step 1 behavior, one to which you must respond, is running off or "bolting."

Two Ways to Respond to Bolting

The best way I have found for families to react to unsafe, scary behaviors is to respond...*but don't react*. In other words, you have to deal with that behavior really quickly and stop it before something bad happens. But you cannot get emotional, or it may get worse. Perhaps this is best illustrated by an example. I will pick on myself, back in 2002, when I was working as a behavior specialist. I had a boy in my classroom whom I'll call Sean who *loved* to get a reaction from me and would do pretty much anything to get one. And at that time, it was not all that hard to do. Sean flushed my watch down the toilet, smashed berries on another boy's back in the woods, and danced on top of his desk to get his classmates riled up. If there was a superpower of getting other people's attention, Sean had it.

After working with Sean for a while, I learned a bit and tried my hardest to ignore any behaviors that I could. But Sean did not like being ignored. So, he decided to test just how patient I could be. One day, Sean ran out of the classroom and bolted for the busy street nearby. I ran after him full speed, yelling and screaming—I was terrified! Sean looked back and laughed as I chased him. I will never forget how scared I was that something would happen to him. Eventually I caught Sean, and he was laughing hysterically, thoroughly enjoying the incredibly strong reactions he was getting from me. I gave Sean a time-out, which he served happily, probably tired from all that running!

Sure enough, the next day, Sean started out being silly and was trying pretty hard to get a reaction from me and his classmates. I kept my cool for a couple of hours. But then, just like the day before, Sean ran out of the classroom as fast as he could, darting toward the street. And once again, I totally lost my cool. I yelled, screamed, threatened a time-out that would last until Sean turned eighteen, and was absolutely beside myself. And when I caught up to Sean, he was laughing hysterically.

As you read this scenario, I hope you were asking yourself, "Why was Sean doing this?" And I also hope that you quickly realized that he was looking for attention. Here I should mention that Sean had other challenges, but he and I had developed a really bad pattern. Sean was used to receiving negative feedback from me—we had a pretty strong *negative* "behavioral momentum." He really liked people and attention and was used to getting negative feedback. So that's what he went after. Over time, we did put into place a much better positive behavior support plan that enabled Sean to earn tokens for good behavior. This shifted his overall behavior so that he no longer was constantly looking for negative attention.

But when Sean was running, what was keeping the behavior going? My reactions, of course. He was getting exactly what he wanted. I have worked with numerous families, often of young children with DS, who also love to run off. Sometimes, this is just because the child sees something cool, such as a beanbag toss game at a carnival that she wants to play. And often children are looking for attention and learn very quickly that this is a good way to get it.

The trouble here is that we cannot ignore bolting. It's not something we can choose not to respond to. We have to do something, or somebody is going to get hurt. With Sean, I had to chase him and bring him back to the safety of the classroom. That much is clear.

But I did not have to lose my cool. I did not have to yell, make eye contact, use strong facial expressions, and rant and rave when Sean ran off. That did not help to keep him safe, help me track him down more quickly, or make him less likely to do the same thing the next day. Instead, my losing my cool made this behavior interesting and fun for Sean. So, not only was my reaction not helpful, it was actually harmful—it made Sean more likely to run off again. I was, in essence, reinforcing his behavior.

When children are engaging in unsafe behaviors, we have to stop the behavior, and fast, to keep everyone safe. But we do not need to lose our cool, because when do, it only tends to make things worse.

Let's use another example to demonstrate how to teach a child not to bolt (a technique that I hadn't developed yet when I had Sean in my class).

Simone was a six-year-old girl with Down syndrome who loved school and was very loving toward her teachers. But whenever her teachers stopped paying attention to her, she ran out of the classroom and bolted for the exit of the building. Of course, Simone's teachers were terrified and ran after her, ranting and raving because they were so scared. And not surprisingly, Simone looked back, laughing and smiling, as her teachers lost their minds!

The teachers initially punished Simone with time-outs and loss of recess time. But this had no effect. She did not seem to understand the connection between running off and receiving a time-out. When we asked her to explain it, she could not.

I suggested to the family and the teachers that they change their strategy. First, we tried to keep the doors closed and as secure as possible without causing a fire hazard. Then, we decided that the teachers would still run after Simone but keep their language very brief and calm: "Simone, stop." They would keep their facial expressions neutral, using a "poker face." When they caught Simone, they agreed to stay calm and neutral. They gave a very brief, simple prompt, "No running," but did not make eye contact, raise their voices, or make strong facial expressions. The teachers practiced looking away and staying neutral. They were going to try to respond…but not react.

So what happened? The next time Simone ran, her teachers kept their emotions in check. They ran after her and said only, "Simone, stop," calmly. When they caught up to her, the teachers took her by the hand, did not look at her, and kept their facial expressions neutral. They did not show how scared and angry they were.

How did Simone react? Well, she didn't find her teachers' new response to her running all that fun. She became a little bit "extra silly" and tried to get a response from them by spitting and making silly noises. But the teachers were ready. They ignored the spitting and silly noises because they knew that this was simply Simone "upping the ante" to try to get a reaction. When they got back to the classroom, Simone clearly wanted some positive attention. Her head teacher looked at her and said calmly, "No running." Then her teacher asked her to "take a break" quietly in the corner, with no games or activities. Simone did not run out of the class for the rest of the day.

Over the next week, Simone ran out of the classroom about half as much as before. Each time, her teachers kept their cool, and when Simone came back, she was required to take a short break. This strategy was hard for the teachers to do, so we should give them a lot of credit! By the second week, Simone seemed to understand that she was not going to get a strong response from her teachers for running away. The behavior had become *boring*. And lo and behold, it stopped.

If we take a moment to reflect upon the changes in Simone's behavior, it is pretty clear what made the difference. It was not that she was made to feel terrible about her behavior, or that she lost a favorite toy or privilege. No, the behavior just wasn't all that much fun anymore. When the teachers took away all of the attention, and more specifically, the response that Simone was receiving for the behavior, it was suddenly not that interesting to her.

So, let's review what is important in how adults respond to a behavior like Simone's. You ***should:***

- Take away eye contact.
- Keep your facial expressions neutral.
- Speak very little, if at all.
- Keep your tone of voice neutral.
- Keep your emotions under control.
- If removing attention and emotions is not enough, then direct the child to "take a break."

And you ***should not:***

- Look right at her.
- Make angry, upset faces.
- Try to explain, using words, why what she did was so horrible.
- Speak in a harsh or animated way.
- Show strong emotions.

Again, when you are disciplining, or responding to a behavior, you have to be very careful about your response. If you have to respond at all, you need to be very thoughtful about how you do it. All those strong reactions you want to have, that your "gut" tells you will work, are really just your own frustration and anger pouring out. Just because you feel that a child should feel bad and upset when you have those reactions does not mean she will. And even if she is upset, it does not mean her behavior will improve. In fact, the behavior usually gets worse. So, you have to respond thoughtfully, without letting your emotions run the show. You have to respond…but not react.

Beyond Discipline: Other Reactive Strategies

When children act out and we cannot prevent it, we automatically begin to think about how to punish them. Many people tell me, "That's how I was raised!" It's true that discipline can be a good way to stop behaviors. What is surprising, though, is that many types of discipline aren't so good for improving behavior over the long term. They may make that behavior stop in the moment it's happening, but it does not mean it won't happen again the next day. Our goal is to help behavior improve, consistently, over time. After all, if we want children with Down syndrome to have the best adult lives possible, we have to help them be their best behaviorally, so problematic behavior does not get in their way.

Here are some strategies other than disciplinary strategies that can help manage behaviors that have already occurred.

Teaching Replacement Behaviors

As I discuss in chapter 5, one of my favorite strategies is teaching replacement behaviors. That is, when a negative behavior occurs, instead of punishing the child for it, we think about why it is occurring and what the child could be doing instead. Here are a couple of examples:

Kiara was a nine-year-old girl with Down syndrome. Every time her class transitioned to the cafeteria or gym, she tried to push her classmates. On a few occasions, she pushed a peer down the stairs. Her teachers tried to explain to Kiara why she should not push other kids and tried punishing her by giving her time-outs and taking away her recess. None of that worked, of course.

When I met with Kiara's family and school staff, I immediately began to think about what else she could be doing besides pushing her classmates.

Did the stairs have a railing? Why yes, of course. Was there a teacher? Yes, of course! Could Kiara hold a railing with one hand and the teacher's hand with the other? Well, they could try it. But why? Well, if both hands are occupied, it's pretty hard to push someone in front of you. The school tried this out, and voilà, the behavior was gone. Of course, her teacher praised her for following the rules of walking on the stairs. And over time, Kiara gradually learned how to safely walk in the halls and on the stairs, so she did not need to hold someone's hand forever. But for managing the immediate behavior, the punishments hadn't worked, and it was impossible to tell classmates who were being pushed to ignore the behavior. So rather than using those strategies, we came up with a replacement behavior for Kiara.

Here's another example. Ryan was a four-year-old preschooler with DS. He loved his classmates and always wanted to play. Ryan was having some trouble with language, however. When he wanted to play with a friend, he struggled with verbally asking them to spend time with him. He was pretty frustrated and was resorting to hitting and pinching his classmates. His classmates didn't like this one bit, and they cried and told the teacher. Ryan didn't like it when they cried, but it seemed to excite him on some level, and he kept pinching and hitting. After all, it was better than getting no response from his classmates! The teachers tried punishing him with time-outs, and they even asked his classmates to ignore the hitting as much as they could. But that doesn't work too well with four-year-olds.

In this case, it was clear that Ryan was having difficulty communicating with his classmates. So, we enlisted the help of Ryan's speech therapist. She began to show him how to tap other children on the shoulder to gain their attention. She also taught Ryan a few signs, like "play with me." The speech therapist even went to the classroom and taught everyone to sign, "I want to play." Ryan practiced quite a bit. His teachers kept an eye on him. When they noticed him looking for a playmate, they reminded him to tap another child on the shoulder or use his signs. And Ryan's friends responded—they often did choose to play with him when he asked instead of pinching! Pretty soon, that behavior had mostly disappeared.

Choosing a Replacement Behavior

To figure out what replacement behaviors to use, it is helpful to go through this checklist:

1. Try to figure out what is motivating the behavior. Ask people who know the child for their theories.
2. If you have a good idea of what the child is trying to accomplish through her behavior, consider these questions: What would be a more appropriate way for her to accomplish that,

given her current level of skills? Who can teach the new skill to her? When and how?
3. If you don't know what is motivating the child, is there a behavior she could do that is incompatible with the problem behavior?
4. Once you identify another behavior the child could do that would accomplish the same goal (e.g., tapping classmates on the shoulder to ask them to play instead of hitting), how will you ensure that the new behavior is consistently reinforced?

Changing the Environment

In addition to planning how to respond to specific behaviors, we can also learn from them and consider ways to change the child's surroundings to help those behaviors decrease. For example, Sophie sneaks out of her bed in the middle of the night and eats all of the ice cream in the freezer. Should you give her a time-out the next day? Of course this is unlikely to help. But putting a lock on the freezer would. Each time Tony gets into the car and his mother starts driving, he unbuckles his seat belt. Again, is it helpful to yell at Tony to put it back (which he cannot do without help)? No, but installing a seatbelt guard and giving Tony a fidget toy to keep his hands occupied would prevent this from happening altogether.

Similarly, I have worked with children who figured out what objects around the house were unsafe and would get a big reaction. For example, one boy learned that taking out a steak knife and chasing his sister around the room would cause a big stir in the house, not surprisingly! His parents had of course tried time-out, speaking with him, and taking away toys, but none of those strategies had worked. When we met, I suggested moving the knives out of his reach. While this may seem like an obvious solution, it is not so easy for families to do. After all, they cooked a lot, and they wanted to teach him about safety in the house. But in the end, they were experiencing so much stress as a family because they were worried about his (and his sister's) safety, that moving the knives was clearly the best option. And it worked.

There are many ways that technology can help us adapt our homes and classrooms to help with behavior and keep people safe. For example, for José, who refuses to stop playing on the iPad, his mother might install an app that turns the tablet off after ten minutes. For children who tend to bolt, there are door alarms and motion sensors that will sound when a person leaves a room. The autism community has also created a very helpful list of tips and technologies to help with wandering and bolting. One such list is provided by Autism Speaks, and can be found at https://www.autismspeaks.org/wandering-resources.

⬤ ⬤ ⬤ ⬤ ⬤ ⬤ ⬤ ⬤ ⬤ ⬤ ⬤ ⬤ ⬤ ⬤ ⬤

Summing Up

Throughout this chapter, I have talked a lot about what we can do after a behavior occurs. These are called "reactive strategies." And I hope that you have come to appreciate that these are not the first option and really not the best choice. Whenever possible, we always want to prevent the behavior in the first place. That's how we know we really understand what the individual with DS is trying to communicate with that behavior. These discipline and "reactive" strategies are really only short-term tools. They may work great when a new behavior pops up, but we should always be trying to figure out what is causing that behavior and trying to prevent it from happening in the first place.

Chapter 9

Times When Behavior Worsens or Changes

Changes in behavior are common for all people, children or adults, with or without neurodevelopmental differences. We all react to changes in the world around us, whether we are aware of it or not. For individuals with Down syndrome, however, these reactions are often more noticeable.

In my experience, there are two types of changes that most often lead to changes in the behavior of someone with Down syndrome: 1) changes in the person's social network and 2) times of transition.

Changes in Relationships

People with DS are often very attuned to other people and really value their relationships with others. So, they can have a hard time dealing with disruptions to their social network. They may have significant behavior changes when confronted with a new teacher, therapist, or classroom aide or when facing more significant losses such as the death of a family member or pet or a divorce in the family. Remember, because people with DS often have very strong social-emotional radar, they are also very sensitive to changes in their relationships with other people.

In addition, people with DS often struggle with language. And language is what many people use to process their difficult feelings. Think about it— when you lose a loved one or go through a difficult change, it is often helpful to talk to someone who understands or at least empathizes. What if speak-

ing were hard for you? What would you do? Again, behavior can be a form of communication. It is a way of telling others, "I'm sad" or "I'm upset."

Although parents and teachers can often predict that children and teenagers with DS will have behavior problems when there are big changes related to key people in their lives, they may not anticipate that more subtle changes or losses can cause pretty major behavior issues. For example, your child might be upset when a favorite cafeteria worker or custodian is no longer around every day to joke around with him and ask him how his day is going or when a classroom aide goes on maternity leave. When behavior becomes a problem, especially out of the blue, we often want to know if there have been any changes in the people who interact with the child that might be related, even if the changes are seemingly small.

As you might know by now, the best way we can help with this type of distress is to prepare the person with DS for changes in relationships and allow him to process the change in a way that works for him. So, depending on his language skills, talking with him about the loss or change may not be very helpful. But creating a Social Story or "good-bye book" that includes information about where that person is going might be very helpful. Further, getting to know the new person who will take the departing person's place could also be helpful in filling this new void.

Transition Times

There are some specific transition times that often seem to lead to behavior issues for children with DS. The most problematic transition seems to be changing schools. For example, leaving preschool or kindergarten and moving into grade school can be a big challenge for some children. Instead of the focus being on playing and interacting with friends, now there is a teacher expecting you to sit in your seat and do work all day. That doesn't sound like fun! Often, when I work with families of young children, I hear complaints about running out of the room, attention-seeking behaviors, and the good old "stop and flop." But now you're a pro, and you know how to handle these! The transitions that seem to surprise more families are when children move from elementary to middle school (or junior high), or directly from a school that includes kindergarten to eighth grade to a high school. I have worked with many children who have done really well in elementary school, with very few behavior problems, lots of friends, and pretty strong academics. The families of many of these children never expected any behavior trouble.

But unfortunately, I have seen many, and heard of many more, children with DS who developed sudden, very problematic behaviors when they moved from elementary to middle or high school. Often, these behaviors include many of those covered earlier in the book, including running away, aggression, and attention-seeking. There may also be other types of behaviors, called internalizing behaviors, which are discussed in the next chapter.

So, why do these behaviors occur? To begin with, a lot of changes happen around middle school. The first is a physical change—many children with DS begin puberty around this time. Puberty can make anybody, whether or not they have DS, more emotional. I have worked with so many children with struggles around this time of life that I wonder if children with DS are even more sensitive to these changes in the body and hormones. Regardless, we can pretty safely assume that the flood of hormones associated with puberty makes children with DS a little more emotional and therefore more likely to act out than before.

But aside from changes in the body, a child's world changes dramatically, both academically and socially, when she moves from elementary to middle school. Let's break this down a bit.

In elementary school, there is a great deal of academic guidance and support. Many assignments are hands-on, and teachers assign projects that have aspects that children find exciting and fun. There is often freedom for children to work together and to do so creatively. Also, when they are younger, many children with DS are not so different from their peers in an academic sense. That is, with supports, children with DS can often participate quite well in academics and classroom activities. (There are, of course, many exceptions; some children struggle more or less academically, and in different subjects). Finally, in elementary school, there is usually just one teacher and one classroom. Sure, students may have a music, art, or even reading teacher. But they have a true "home base" with a homeroom teacher, and the routine is pretty clear.

Much of this changes in middle school. First, children are expected to sit and work on academics all day, pretty independently. There may be occasional projects and group work, but much of the school day involves sitting at a desk alone. This independent learning style is not ideally suited to people with Down syndrome. Next, this is often the age when developmental differences between students with and without disabilities become more apparent. Over time, the gap between what students with and without DS can do becomes larger as both groups make progress, but at different speeds. As if this is not frustrating enough for the person with DS, the school day becomes filled with transitions. Instead of having one teacher, students generally have many teachers, with classrooms spread out across a big school. For children who have done well in inclusion classrooms, this transition can be particularly hard, because the school day is becoming far less structured.

There are also major shifts in the social scene between elementary school and middle school. In elementary school, children and their parents are often less selective when inviting classmates to an event. If there's a birthday party, some kids invite everyone in the class, particularly in the lower grades. At recess, adults encourage all the students to play together nicely and intervene if they don't. When children play T-ball or soccer, everyone wins a trophy. Parents set up playdates and arrange the activities. There is a structure and predictability to friendships that really benefits all children, including those with DS.

When children move to middle school, those relationships become much more complex. Instead of a parent organizing all the kids to play kickball every Saturday at the park, the children themselves might agree to go play videogames at someone's house after school, without a parent's help. If a child with DS is not part of that conversation, he is likely to be excluded. When children move on to middle school, relationships also become much more focused on shared interests and talents. The football players spend time together, the chess club spends time together, and the dance troupe spends time together. The children are often very focused on their skills and can be quite competitive. What if those skills are harder for you? It does not mean that your friends do not want to spend time with you, but you might end up feeling left out anyway. This is also a period when fitting in matters a lot, and typically developing children and teens are often less likely to want to be associated with students who are obviously different. And bullying of students with differences often ramps up after elementary school.

For all of these reasons, school transitions can result in first-time behavior problems for some children with DS or worsening behaviors for others.

Making School Transitions Easier

The first step in helping a child with DS deal with school transitions is for parents and teachers to always be aware. If you know this is a time that behavior can become an issue, you are already far better prepared. And as you know, when we are paying attention to something, anything, we can usually cause it to change. Beyond awareness, however, there are some pretty basic strategies that seem to really work.

What works for people with Down syndrome:

- predictability
- structure
- visuals

What doesn't work for people with Down syndrome:

- an unpredictable environment, or not knowing what to expect
- lack of routine and structure
- having explanations given with speech alone

If you review the lists above, it is no wonder that transitions to middle or high school can cause some trouble. After all, everything is different! There are far more transitions, much less structure, and a lot more complicated social relationships, which revolve around pretty advanced language. What a nightmare!

But there are some ways to help. Let's start with predictability. If a child or adolescent with DS is about to change schools or experience any other big change, for that matter, I often think of it as if they are entering an abyss. You may remember the movie by the same name from the 1980s in which older people entered a very mysterious world underwater and had no idea what to expect. For people with DS, school transitions may be similar. They do not know what to expect, and people try to help with that by *explaining* it with language.

So, the first step with any big transition is to provide a real-world sense of what's coming. And what better way to do that than by visiting the new school? Amanda, a twelve-year-old with DS who is going to be moving to the middle school next year, could visit her new building, meet her homeroom teacher, see her homeroom, learn about lockers, and see where her various classes are going to be. Sounds like fun. Now imagine the alternative, which is usually to have a parent or teacher say something like this: "Now, Amanda, next year you will be going to middle school in a new building. You will have a lot of different teachers. Your homeroom (whatever that means!) teacher will be Mr. Simmons. You'll have a locker to put all of your stuff in."

You can imagine how anxiety-provoking this verbal description of a mysterious new place would be for any child. For people with DS, it provokes much more anxiety. Change is really hard for all of the reasons discussed previously. And beyond that, when adults try to explain changes that are coming, language may not help at all. I have worked with many families for whom it seems that language actually makes things *worse*.

In addition to having the child visit his new school, I like to add in Social Stories. We know that processing new information can be hard and that having many chances to learn that information can help a great deal. So, when children are visiting their new school, I suggest taking some pictures of the building, the teachers, and better yet, the child in that building and with those teachers. You can then put all of those pictures into a book and read it several times over the summer. When families do this, by the time a child enters his new school, he knows all about it. He can usually tell anyone who will listen all about his teachers, his homeroom, his locker, and any other details.

When we know what is coming, we all feel less anxious. A great deal of the refusal and "stop and flop" that we all have seen in children and even adolescents with DS is, in my opinion, due to fear. If I don't know what's coming next, I'm going to feel afraid. And if I feel afraid, I am going to avoid that thing that is so scary, whatever it may be.

For many families, making some visits and creating a Social Story has been invaluable. These strategies help children and adolescents with DS to understand and remember what will be coming down the road. And that dramatically reduces anxiety. And when that anxiety is reduced, behavior is much, much better.

Considering the Peer Group

A while back, I presented a talk about behavior challenges when individuals with DS transition to middle or high school at a national conference for professionals. I presented the ideas discussed above, and most people thought they sounded pretty helpful. However, Terri Couwenhoven, author of the invaluable book, *Teaching Children with Down Syndrome about their Bodies, Boundaries, and Sexuality: A Guide for Parents and Professionals*, made an excellent point. (This point has also been made by Dr. Dennis Maguire and Dr. Brian Chicoine, who wrote the outstanding book, *Mental Wellness in Adults with Down Syndrome*.)

Terri commented that often in elementary school, children with DS are so successfully included that they may not make good friends with other children with special needs. Many families think this is a great thing—their child with DS is a part of the community, regardless of his neurodevelopmental status. But when children transition to middle and high school, relationships with peers can change quite a bit. And if those relationships don't last, or simply change a lot, it can be very hard for the child or teen with DS, as it would be for anyone. Terri suggested that it is important to make friends with peers in both the typically developing community and the disability community to protect against this. And I think it's an excellent point. In fact, I now recommend this as part of my "transition to middle or high school package" for families.

Another way that I conceptualize this is to think of a spider web. We all have stress in our lives, and we all need connections. The more connections a spider web has, the stronger it is, and the more stress it can take. Similarly, for anyone, including children and teens with DS, the more connections in the world the better, and the more stress they will be able to tolerate.

There are many ways to form relationships in the disability community. You might set up activities with other children who have disabilities, or ask teachers and the special education coordinator if there are other kids that your child sees at school who might make a good friend outside of school. Even if there are no other compatible students the same age in your school system (which makes finding friends easiest, of course), the Special Olympics, local ARC chapters, and local chapters of Down syndrome or disability advocacy groups often offer social activities for children, teens, and families.

Chapter 10

Managing Internalizing Behaviors in Adolescence

Adolescence can be a very challenging time for anyone. We all remember some of our struggles at this point in our lives. Teens and young adults with Down syndrome are not exempt from these struggles. As discussed above, changes in the body, school, and peer relationships can take a real toll. And for many, that can lead to behavior problems.

The behaviors I have discussed so far in the book have been mostly "acting out" behaviors. We call these "externalizing behaviors," because they involve someone acting in a way that affects the environment around her, such as hitting or destroying property. But during adolescence, we also start to see, often for the first time, what we refer to as "internalizing behaviors." This refers to "acting in," or symptoms such as anxiety or depression in which the person becomes more withdrawn or lethargic or appears not to be interested in activities and other people.

Unfortunately, anxiety and depression are relatively common in people with DS, starting in adolescence and becoming even more common in adulthood. This may be due to differences in the brain and body, stress related to having trouble with learning or development, or other factors that we don't yet understand.

Anxiety and depression in children and teens with DS can look a bit different than you might imagine. For example, instead of being sad, crying, and not wanting to get out of bed, some people with DS who become depressed may begin to speak far less clearly, lose some toileting skills, or wish to stay in their bedroom and watch videos instead of talking with friends or family members. If this sounds like something your child or teen is struggling with, I strongly recommend the book, *Mental Wellness in Adults with Down Syn-*

drome, by Dennis McGuire and Brian Chicoine. It's an incredible book that, despite its primary focus on adults, is very helpful to families of children and teens struggling with these issues as well.

It is beyond the scope of this book to go into all of the details about mental health challenges in people with DS. It is important, however, that if you notice some key symptoms, you take your child or teen to the doctor or a mental health specialist to be evaluated and treated. These symptoms include the following:

- isolating oneself from friends and family
- losing interest in activities the person used to enjoy
- having very little energy
- speaking less, or being harder to understand
- crying for no reason
- losing skills or having toileting accidents after being potty trained

In addition, major shifts in behavior can also occur when a young person is being harmed and does not know how to get help. Physical and sexual abuse as well as bullying can also result in behavioral changes, and if you have concerns about any of these, please seek professional help (see chapter 12).

Common Behavior Changes in Teens with Down Syndrome

Again, addressing all of the possible mental health challenges of individuals with DS is well beyond what we can hope to cover in this book. But besides the more concerning health problems such as anxiety or depression, many individuals with DS start to exhibit more minor internalizing behaviors as they enter puberty and into the teen years.

It can be hard for parents to figure out whether to be concerned about their child's behavior or not, so you may want to talk with your child's doctor if you are not sure. But, assuming you have been able to determine that your child is not experiencing a true mental health challenge, you still may observe some new behaviors, including the following:

- wanting to spend more time alone, particularly after a long day at school
- more talking to herself
- engaging in imaginary play that you haven't seen in a few years or more
- watching certain videos or songs over and over again

Each of these behaviors can be concerning or frustrating for a parent. After all, you love your child dearly and want to spend time together as a family. So why is she, all of a sudden, spending so much time alone?

Let's start with a reminder that this is pretty typical behavior for teens. It is completely normal and expected for teenagers to want to spend less time with parents and more time alone or with friends. So, teens and young adults with DS also often withdraw from their parents, and it is not necessarily a problem.

The other piece of this puzzle that is specific to Down syndrome is again that "gas in the tank" idea discussed in chapter 2. Remember, we all have a certain amount of mental energy (or gas in the tank) for our day. If a person has difficulty with any aspect of her day, such as learning, language, or social skills, that gas is being used up faster than for someone who does not have those challenges.

When a child with DS becomes a teenager, lots of things become harder. As we discussed above, there are changes in the body, in school, and with friends. So, for many teens, the gas in the tank is being used up pretty fast, day after day.

If you think about the gas in the tank theory, is it still surprising that many teens with DS want to spend time alone after school? Many seem to need a break from all the language, social demands, and academics that exhausted them throughout the day. And that is perfectly okay. In other words, we as adults do not need to force teens with DS to interact after school, to leave their rooms, or to do what they "used to do" after a long day. In fact, in my experience, forcing someone with DS to do so can be harmful and can make teens with DS more anxious or withdrawn.

So, this becomes a balancing act. You have to consider how much time your teen may need to unwind and whether spending time alone is causing any harm. For many, an hour or two of alone time at some point in the afternoon or evening can really help to recharge the mental battery. After that time, many teens with DS will happily engage with family members or friends. (If the teen never wants to reengage with others, however, it may be wise to investigate whether she has a more serious problem such as anxiety or depression.)

So, some downtime is not necessarily a bad thing for teens with DS. But what about the other behaviors mentioned above: talking to oneself, becoming a bit obsessed with certain songs or videos, or engaging in pretend play that you would expect in a much younger child?

Actually, as I've worked with more teens with DS, I've come to believe these behaviors are pretty normal for people with Down syndrome. Most professionals believe these behaviors are ways of processing all that has happened during a busy day.

For example, if fifteen-year-old Jasmine is attending high school with many different peers and teachers, she is probably hearing and seeing a lot during the day. As we know, processing all of that information, and particularly language, can be pretty challenging. One way that the brain can deal with that is to replay those interactions after the dust has settled. So, is it really all that surprising when Jasmine comes home, goes to her room, and either repeats some of those conversations to herself or acts them out with her stuffed animals? For many with DS, these sorts of behaviors seem to help them process the day, and perhaps, more importantly, decompress and relax.

Some teens with DS do not need or want to repeat everything that has happened throughout the day. Instead, they want to do the same thing over and over again until they settle down. For many, this involves watching a particular video or part of a video over and over again. Others may decompress by twirling a piece of string or spinning around a bit in their bedroom. Parents are often confused by these repetitive behaviors and some worry that they may be a sign of something else, such as autism. However, for many children and teens with DS, doing something over and over again is simply soothing. It is a way to relieve stress and settle down. If your child engages in repetitive behaviors, ask yourself these questions: When your child does the behavior, does she seem to be more relaxed? Does she do it primarily when stressed or tired? If your answer to these questions is *yes,* these behaviors are not necessarily problematic.

To determine whether one of these types of behaviors is problematic, I recommend that you revisit Ross Greene's steps of ignoring (see chapter 8). Ask yourself: Is this a safety issue? If so, intervene, of course (and remember to respond...*but don't react!*). If it is not a safety issue, is it one of the top three behaviors you are concerned about? If not, it's probably best to leave it alone. If yes, then you can try some strategies to deal with it, but proceed with caution and read below. Is the behavior simply something that you don't like, but that is doing no harm? If so, you should probably ignore it.

Deciding Whether an Internalizing Behavior Is a Problem

How do we know whether an internalizing behavior, like spending time alone or self-talk, is a problem? Remember what Frued said: *something is only a problem if it interferes with one's ability to love or work*. For a child or teenager, I change his definition of a problem a bit to the following: *something is only a problem if it interferes with one's ability to socialize and to learn*. After all, the jobs of children and teens are to interact with others and to learn.

So, internalizing behaviors are only a problem if they get in the way of those activities.

For Alicia, age sixteen, isolating behaviors may not be a problem if she goes to her room for an hour after school to watch YouTube videos but then comes out to play with her little sister and neighbor and then has dinner with her family. She may even engage in some self-talk or act out some of her day with toys in her room. If Alicia is learning and making some progress in school and interacting with her family and friends, there really is not any reason to stop her from spending some downtime alone in her room.

Now let's think about Benjamin, age fourteen, who is going to his room after school and playing a video game for hours on end. He is refusing to come out and chat with family members and only comes out for dinner because he is hungry. During dinner, Benjamin only wants to talk about his game, and his teachers have been sending home notes complaining that he is drawing pictures of Minecraft in school instead of doing his schoolwork and participating in class. For Benjamin, there seems to be a problem. His intense focus on his video game is interfering with his interactions with family and friends and is also getting in the way of his learning.

What should Benjamin's parents do? As you may guess at this point in the book, they need to provide some structure. Benjamin clearly needs some limits with videogames, and having as much time as he wants in his own room is not working very well. So, Benjamin's parents wisely decide to move his computer into the family room, and they install a timer app that only allows thirty minutes of game time per day. Benjamin is still able to play his game and unwind, but not all day long. And sure enough, he begins to engage more with his friends and family, and his schoolwork improves.

I should say here that for some children, a focus on a particular game or movie, or even a certain peer, can become very intense, to the point of an obsession. There have been several times when I have recommended that parents find creative ways to take away a game or video because a child or teen cannot stop focusing on it. Of course, you have to come up with a way of doing this that will be effective. For example, I worked with a teenage boy, Ravi, who became really focused on Eminem, the rapper. The problem was that he became so obsessed with Eminem that he began to get really upset when he listened to the music and felt so horrible for all the things the rapper had to endure in his early life. He would cry and speak about this all the time, to the point that it interfered with his school work. Of course, we could not simply take away Eminem. So, his parents and I worked with Ravi to find some sports games and other music that he found to be cool. We agreed that he could have these other games and music, but we would delete the Eminem from his iPod. Sure enough, within a few days, Ravi stopped focusing so much on Eminem and was able to talk about other topics. He also seemed happier and less stressed.

The good news is that restricting an activity that the teen is overly focused on usually seems to work, and the individual usually moves on to other more productive activities pretty quickly. But it does take some creative thinking, and you will likely have to replace the obsession with something else that's more productive or less harmful.

Self-Talk

The same strategies can be used for other internalizing behaviors. For example, many families have spoken with me about self-talk. It is well documented that people with developmental challenges often struggle to develop "internal dialogue." That is, the ability to think through conversations and interactions, or even practice them, as we all do, without actually saying them out loud. So, it is important to know that talking out loud to oneself is really not a major problem in itself. Still, if someone with DS talks to herself all through the day and it is puzzling or disruptive to peers or others, it can cause some social problems.

We have to be careful that we do not try to take this behavior away or punish the person for it, because it is a healthy and normal way of processing what's happening in the world. For many families, what works is to limit the behavior and put a structure around it.

Many families try to structure self-talk by limiting it to times or places in which it will cause few or no problems. For example, sixteen-year-old Will was engaging in self-talk throughout the day. This led his friends in school to leave him out of conversations and activities. Since self-talk was limiting Will's social life, it was most likely a problem. What should Will's family do? Should they punish Will or ignore his self-talk? Neither was a great option. It wouldn't be wise to punish Will for something that is healthy and may help him process the world around him. But his parents also did not want to ignore a behavior that was limiting his social life.

Instead, Will's family and teachers made some ground rules. They talked with Will (using language that he understood; you could also use visuals) and agreed that self-talk would be reserved for times when he was in his bedroom after school. And if he really needed to unwind in school, he could ask for a break in the guidance counselor's office, where he could also do some self-talk. The counselor was careful to limit this break to only a few minutes, made sure it was not too much fun, and ensured that he did not give Will so much attention that he would want to do this all day, every day. The school also made sure that Will made up any work that he missed while with the guidance counselor so that he did not use this as a way to avoid doing his schoolwork. Will and his family agreed on a signal—buttoning their lips—to remind him to wait to engage in self-talk until he was in the right place, at the right time.

You might ask yourself how and why Will agreed to this plan. Well, the most important piece of that puzzle is that he was involved in making the plan! Will spoke with his parents and his teachers about self-talk and agreed that it was causing him to be left out at school. He was asked what could be done, and, with some help, Will came up with the idea of limiting self-talk to his room or the counselor's office. He even helped decide on the reminder signal of buttoning his lip. So, from Will's perspective, this was really *his* plan. And just as with visual schedules and token economies, if we can allow the child or teen to be a part of creating a plan, he or she is far more likely to buy in and participate.

Of course, if a person is unwilling to change this behavior or does not see it as a problem, you may have to become more creative. You might teach a teen with DS to whisper so that self-talk doesn't interfere so much in her school day. For example, you could play a game in which she and her parents or teacher each try to talk more softly than the other, If the teen is concerned about how others view her, you might try videotaping her talking to herself to help her understand the issue and become more motivated to address it.

• • • • • • • • • • • • • • •

Summing Up

Regardless of the specific behavioral issue or the actual method of dealing with it, hopefully, the main message of this chapter is apparent. That is, internalizing behaviors, or "acting in," are very common in teens with DS. In fact, I expect them to happen, as you would with any other teenager. They are only a problem if they are getting in the way of other things. If they are not getting in the way, it is usually best to leave them alone. If internalizing problems *are* getting in the way of learning or socializing, then it is best to build in some structure, exchange them for another behavior that meets the same need, and to limit them, but not to take them away completely. After all, every behavior has a function, and we need to respect that a teen's *acting in* behavior is simply her way of telling us what she needs.

Chapter 11

Maintaining Behavior Gains over the Long Term

At this point in the book, I hope you are feeling like an expert in understanding behavior challenges in individuals with DS and strategies for managing them. For most families, having a bit of understanding of why these behaviors occur and learning some basic strategies goes a long way. But many families are left with these questions: How can we keep this up? What do we do when the next behavior issue arises? These are great questions. After all, I often tell families that behavior management is a bit like *Whack-a-Mole*. Each time you address one behavior, another one eventually pops up.

The first—and perhaps most important—thing to remember when you are considering how to manage your child's behaviors over the long term is that all behaviors serve a purpose. Behaviors are not happening just to drive us adults nuts. If you step back and consider why a behavior is happening, you have a much better chance of responding effectively. Remember how powerful ignoring an attention-seeking behavior can be?

Second, you have to think about what to respond to and what

to ignore. When new behaviors emerge, always ask yourself: Is this really a problem? Or is this just annoying? For example, if your teenager develops a new habit of humming incessantly, is this something that you want to lose your mind over? If the humming is not limiting his ability to do his school-work and interact with friends, then it's probably best to let it go. If you can't ignore it altogether, perhaps try to limit it to a certain time of day or to a place such as your child's bedroom.

Perhaps you are facing a new problem that just suddenly emerged. For example, when you were at the grocery store, your ten-year-old girl took a pack of gum without paying, or even worse, your fifteen-year-old boy patted a woman's rear end! Again, I would encourage you to stop and think before reading further. Now that you know a great deal about the brain and behavior in DS, what will work and what will not? In both of these situations, you do have to respond. You cannot ignore steal-ing or inappropriate touching, of course! But your natural instinct is going to be to respond with a lot of intensity and emotion. After all, you are probably embarrassed and perhaps a bit scared. But remember, showing strong emo-tional reactions will probably not help matters. Even worse, they may seem fun or exciting to your child or teenager. So, again, remember to respond… *but don't react.*

If your child steals, try to stay very calm and collected and require him to walk back into the store and return the gum to the clerk, hopefully with-out penalty. You can use some brief coaching here, but remember to keep the words to a minimum. Perhaps say something such as "Pay first, then take gum." But you have to remember to stay calm, or you will turn this new steal-ing behavior into something fun, and then it will be more likely to happen again. If you child already chewed the gum, and if he can understands the cause and effect, you may wish to give him the money to pay for it and then ask him to do a job when he gets home to "earn" the gum. But this will only be effective if the child understands. In the moment, the most important thing is to keep your cool, but still call him out on the negative behavior.

For the patting of a stranger's rear end, which would surely be mortify-ing, it is even more important to stay calm, just when it is hardest! In this situ-ation, you may need to start by asking your teen to sit on a bench and "take a break." During that time, you will probably need to speak to the stranger and apologize for the behavior. Hopefully, that will be the end of it. (But if it persists, see the next chapter about other resources, such as schools and sexual education, for help). Then, with a calm face and tone of voice, you want to provide a reminder to your teen, "No touching strangers." Remember, as tempting as it would be to become very upset or even yell, this would prob-ably have the negative consequence of making the behavior seem that much

more fun and interesting. Best to keep calm, gather your thoughts, and consider whether this is a behavior that you will have to deal with again or just a one-time occurrence. If it's a recurring theme, you'll probably need to ask for some help, as discussed in the next chapter.

Perhaps the biggest stumbling block for most families is assuming that as a child gets older, the strategies won't be necessary or won't work any longer. For example, I have worked with many families who were struggling with the morning routine or transitions. Many of these families have had great success with visual schedules, First-Then, and token economies/chore charts. I often do not see them for years on end while behavior is going well. However, I also often receive calls and emails about new behaviors from families who are very upset because they thought they were "done with behavior issues."

While I can certainly understand these families' points of view, if you understand the brain in Down syndrome, you won't be surprised to learn that behavior issues can crop up at any age. Even though individuals grow older, the same brain-based differences remain. Language is usually still challenging, visuals still work best, motivation can continue to be an issue, and routine works well, but change is hard. So, when new behaviors come up, or new times of the day become challenging, I very often suggest to parents that they go back to the basics.

For many adolescents and adults with disabilities, a visual schedule, list, or reminders on an iPhone, iPad, or other smartphone or tablet remain invaluable tools that help them get through the day. Similarly, token economies or chore charts are powerful for anyone. Think about it—doesn't getting paid at work help you be more motivated? Doesn't it feel good to receive that paycheck? Of course, as people with DS grow and mature, we have to change the pictures, or jobs, and the rewards. We have to make sure they are interesting and motivating for the child or adolescent. But the same principles still apply.

The same is true for punishment. As many with DS continue to be very sociable as adolescents and adults, those same attention-seeking tendencies remain. And the social-emotional radar is still highly attuned. So, even as people with DS mature, parents, teachers, therapists, and others need to be very careful about their own reactions and realize that they remain powerful tools for shaping and managing behavior.

As you encounter new behaviors and try to keep the positive behaviors going over time, also remember that flexibility is key. When you find yourself facing new behaviors that concern you, remember that it is tempting to become angry and rigid and to stick to the "rules," whatever they may be. It can be tempting to think first about how to punish your child or teen for a new behavior, and you may not even realize you are becoming angry and inflexible. But remember, not only does this tend not to work very well, but it can also be really counterproductive. Your child or adolescent will sense your anger, and it may make the behavior seem more fun or interesting, increasing the likelihood that it will keep happening. And remember, all of that emotion is hard on your relationship, the most important thing of all.

So, when you are facing a new behavior, perhaps the most important thing to do is to stop and take a deep breath. Think about what you are seeing and why it is happening. You are probably far more skilled at this than you think. It may help to talk it over with a spouse, colleague, or a friend and try to figure out why the behavior is happening. Is your child seeking attention, trying to escape something unpleasant, trying to meet some need or get something he or she wants? Depending on the answer, you will have some ideas about how to respond to the behavior, and more importantly how to prevent it in the future.

If you find yourself being inflexible or rigid in your approach to a behavior, especially if that approach is not working, I encourage you to return to this book and read through a couple of chapters. You might also want to chat with a friend or colleague who is not directly involved. Sometimes, it is hard to see things clearly when you are stuck in the middle and feeling emotional. Talking with a friend can help you clear your head and think with less emotion.

Chapter 12

Where to Turn for Help: Professional Resources

Throughout this book, we have talked a great deal about how to understand behaviors and what you can do to manage them yourself. Hopefully, you are feeling pretty positive and excited about all of the ways that you can support positive behavior. But at some point, you might face behavior challenges that you cannot manage on your own. It may be that there is something else going on with your child or teen—such as a medical or psychiatric condition that affects behavior. Or, it may be that these strategies just are not working for you and your family. Whatever the reason, there are many resources available to assist with behavior. This chapter provides you with a basic overview of these options.

The Pediatrician and Other Health Care Providers

Just as with any other issue affecting your child or adolescent's well-being, the pediatrician or primary care doctor is a good place to start. The doctor may be able to screen for some conditions that could affect behavior. The doctor may feel comfortable assessing these issues herself, or she may wish to refer you to a specialist for further evaluation. There are Down syndrome specialty clinics across the country, including at my home at Boston Children's Hospital. Some of the medical issues that could affect behavior include the following:

- pain (ears, dental, gastrointestinal, bones, headache, menstrual)
- infections

- sleep disorders (due to sleep apnea, medication side effects, behavioral issues)
- nutrition (such as food sensitivities)
- hearing or vision impairment
- celiac disease
- thyroid disease
- gastrointestinal problems (such as constipation, reflux, abdominal pain)

If medical issues have been evaluated and do not seem to be the cause of the behavior challenges, your child's doctor may want to send him or her to meet with a specialist. The specialist may be a psychologist, psychiatrist, developmental and behavioral pediatrician, or a neurologist. While many specialists have experience working with people with DS or similar developmental disabilities, many do not. Many will have completed specialized training in areas such as neurodevelopment, neurodevelopmental disabilities, pediatric psychology, or neuropsychology. It is probably best to ask if the specialist has some experience with DS. However, if the person does not, he or she still may be a good fit. Often, professionals who have experience with other conditions such as autism, intellectual disability, or other genetic syndromes may have good, relevant skills.

Any healthcare professional that you consult will want to understand exactly what challenges you are seeing, with examples. He or she will want to know when these problems started and whether there were any other challenges facing your child and family at that time. Healthcare providers will also want to know how these behaviors have progressed over time and whether anything has made them better or worse, as well as what happens immediately before and after the behavior. If you can gather your thoughts and make some notes about these basics before your visit, you are likely to get the most out of your conversation.

Many healthcare providers will want to do their own evaluation. As a pediatric psychologist specializing in neurodevelopment, I often conduct neuropsychological testing with my patients. I am able to measure a child's or adolescent's cognitive skills, learning, memory, language abilities, social skills, motor functions, and behavior. I also ask families for a great deal of information about therapies and school programming. This allows me to determine if there may be another diagnosis, such as ADHD or autism, contributing to behavior. It also allows me to assess whether the environment may be an issue. For example, is the child's school and therapeutic program tailored to her needs?

If you are seeing a physician who specializes in Down syndrome, you may end up discussing medications that can be helpful. While this can be scary for families, medications can often be very helpful for challenges such as anxiety, depression, or impulsive, aggressive, or obsessive behaviors. Of course, it is important to make sure that a thorough evaluation is done to figure out what the problems are. And the physician will then be sure to monitor your child for effects, and side effects, of the medication. The good news is that I have seen many children respond very positively to medications, so try not to let fear of medicines for behavior get the best of you. After all, if a doctor told you that your child needed medicine for anything happening below your child's neck, you probably would not hesitate to give her the medicine. Why is medicine related to behavior, anxiety, or mood any different? In my opinion, it's not. It's really just a cultural phenomenon that we consider these different.

If you are looking for a Down syndrome specialist, you might try looking into the National Down Syndrome Society's database: http://www.ndss.org/Resources/Health-Care/Health-Care-Providers. We also have many resources available through Boston Children's Hospital and our own Down Syndrome Program website: www.BostonChildrens.org/DownSyndrome.

Home Behavior Providers

Depending on where you live and what type of health insurance plan you have, you may be able to get assistance from home-based behavior providers. Typically, these are behaviorists who are college graduates and are supervised by a more senior clinician or behaviorist (e.g., a psychologist or someone who specializes in applied behavior analysis and has certification from the Behavior Analyst Certification Board, a BCBA).

Home-based behavior providers typically visit families one to three times per week. Usually, home-based services focus on training the adults in the home how to manage a child's behaviors. They usually begin by conducting an assessment, sometimes a functional behavior assessment (FBA), as described below. Then, a plan is developed to help the family and the child do their best with behavior. Typically, a child or adolescent has to have a diagnosis of a condition that affects behavior from a professional, such as ADHD or disruptive behavior disorder, to receive these services. So, you may have to see your doctor or a specialist as a first step.

The School

Schools can be a big help when it comes to behavior management of children and adolescents with disabilities. Behavior is part of a child's development, and in the United States, the federal Individuals with Disabilities Education Act (IDEA) provides very specific guidance on assessment of behavior problems and interventions. When behavior is a problem at school or at home, a good first step is talking to the teacher. Does she see this behavior in the classroom? Does she have any ideas about what works and what does not?

You may get some great information just from having a conversation.

Beyond just talking with the school personnel, you can also request help with behavior from specialists in the school. When children are struggling with behavior, schools can often provide some assessment of the problem.

Functional behavior assessment, or FBA, is a standardized way of gathering information about what happens before (antecedent), during (behavior), and after a behavior (the consequence). Some people refer to this as the ABCs of behavior. The best FBAs are performed by trained behaviorists, such as a psychologist or a board certified behavior analyst (BCBA). Regardless of who does the assessment, the person must be trained in conducting FBAs. He or she should not only spend time observing the child's behavior at school, but also at home and in the community. This will allow the behaviorist to learn if certain environments make the behavior better or worse. Through an FBA, we can determine how often a behavior is happening and what may be causing it or reinforcing it. The FBA can also keep track of how often a behavior is occurring and can be used to set up a system for monitoring changes in behavior, for better or for worse, over time.

But what good is an assessment of behavior if the school or family doesn't know what to do about it? I'm so glad you asked! Unfortunately, I have seen many children who have had FBAs conducted but do not have behavior plans at school. In other words, someone took the time to extensively evaluate their behavior but then did not come up with a plan to help. What a waste! Of course, if a child has an FBA, she should also have a plan.

Behavior Intervention Plans (BIP), Behavior Support Plans (BSP), and Positive Behavior Support Plans (PBSP) (these terms are often used interchangeably) are behavior plans that are based on an FBA or another assessment of an individual's behavior. In other words, they are tailored to the child. Behavior plans should be developed by the behavior specialist and/or school-based psychologist. They should take into account feedback from parents and teachers. Behavior plans should be shared with all staff and the family, so that everyone can be using the same strategies consistently. I prefer for the specifics of a behavior plan to be described in the IEP, though this often does not happen. Still, the IEP should have behavior both as a goal and an intervention, even if the specifics of the behavior plan are not included. In addition, families should receive regular feedback about how the behavior plan is working. The school should send home daily or weekly "report cards" noting how the day went. It is important to include both positive aspects of the day and challenges. Parents need to be able to praise their child for doing well and not just focus on things that go poorly. If you recall, we referred to this earlier as "differential reinforcement."

The best BIPs have mostly "proactive strategies." That is, they focus on encouraging the child's good behaviors and on preventing negative behaviors. They usually involve using visual aids, token economies, replacement behaviors, and the other tools that we spent most of this book discussing. Usually, BIPs also have some "reactive strategies." Hopefully, these do not focus too much on punishing and all the problematic ways of dealing with behaviors you know to avoid. Ideally, the reactive strategies should be focused on ignoring or redirecting the child when negative behaviors occur or on effective discipline techniques such as time-out or taking breaks. And of course, everyone should stay calm and respond…*but don't react.*

Sometimes, schools offer behavior support outside of the classroom. For example, some schools will send a behaviorist to a family's home if there are a lot of problems in that setting. I have seen this when children refuse to get onto the bus or have unsafe behaviors in the home. Often, this type of home behavior support is focused on training the adults in the house to use effective strategies such as those discussed in this book.

Schools can also offer support for specific issues that may arise at particular times. For example, as discussed in chapter 9, behaviors can become challenging when a child transitions to a new school. Often, the school can help a family prepare the child with visits, Social Stories, and other strategies tailored to that child. Further, schools can help by providing education on specific issues. The most common example is sexual education. For many individuals with DS, going through puberty and discovering sexuality can be challenging. They may have difficulties understanding what sexual behaviors are okay and when to engage in them. Again, I strongly recommend the book, *Teaching Children with Down Syndrome about Their Bodies, Boundaries, and Sexuality: A Guide for Parents and Professionals,* by Terri Couwenhoven.

Schools usually prefer to use a specific curriculum for sexual education. The curriculum that I have found most successful for individuals with DS is the *Circles* curriculum (http://www.stanfield.com/products/family-life-relationships/social-skills-circles-curriculum-intimacy-relationships/). Unfortunately, some schools may only offer students with DS or other developmental challenges the typical sexual education curriculum, or none at all. Neither strategy tends to work very well. After all, people with DS are going to experience sexual feelings like anyone else, and they need to understand these feelings and how to act on them safely.

Chapter 13

Conclusion

Throughout this book, we have talked a great deal about behaviors, about how important you are as a caregiver, and how we can help children and adolescents with Down syndrome do their best behaviorally. And throughout all of these conversations, I hope that one thing has been clear — your relationship with your child is the most important thing of all.

Hopefully, as you have read these chapters, learned about effective strategies to manage behavior, and thought about how you might apply them, you have also learned ways to make things go more smoothly in your home or your classroom. If so, you have also learned how to lessen the stress on the relationship between you and your child or student with DS. As discussed at the start of this book, that relationship is special. By maintaining a positive relationship with your child or student, you don't just keep everyone happier. You also help each other regulate stress, manage frustration, and be healthier. Of course, this book does not cover every possible behavior problem or intervention under the sun. Instead, I hope you have learned to think about behavior in a constructive way that lets you, a newly minted behavior expert, think creatively about how to manage the behaviors you are facing.

Remember, when behavior is causing problems in your home or classroom, think about what will be best for your relationship with the child or teen who is struggling. Respond thoughtfully to his or her behaviors, based on understanding what this other person is trying to tell you through his or her behavior. And watch out for those gut reactions. This is the best way to improve behavior over the long term. And that is how you respond...*but don't react.*

Suggested Reading

The list below includes the publications I've referenced in the preceding chapters as well as a few other titles that you may want to consult for further information about topics discussed in the book.

Barkley, Russell. *Taking Charge of ADHD: The Complete Authoritative Guide for Parents*. 3rd ed. New York: Guilford Press, 2013.

Cooper-Kahn, Joyce, and Laurie Dietzel. *Late, Lost, and Unprepared: A Parents' Guide to Helping Children with Executive Functioning*. Bethesda, MD: Woodbine House, 2008.

Couwenhoven, Terri. *Teaching Children with Down Syndrome about Their Bodies, Boundaries, and Sexuality: A Guide for Parents and Professionals*. Bethesda, MD: Woodbine House, 2007.

Fidler, Deborah, and Lynn Nadel. "Education and Children with Down Syndrome: Neuroscience, Development, and Intervention. *Mental Retardation and Developmental Disabilities Research Reviews* 13 (2007): 262–71.

Glasberg, Beth. *Functional Behavior Assessment for People with Autism: Making Sense of Seemingly Senseless Behavior*. 2nd ed. Bethesda, MD: Woodbine House, 2015.

Gray, Carol. *The New Social Story Book: Over 150 Social Stories That Teach Everyday Social Skills to Children and Adults with Autism and Their Peers*. Rev. ed. Arlington, TX: Future Horizons, 2015.

Greene, Ross. *The Explosive Child: A New Approach for Understanding and Parenting Easily Frustrated, Chronically Inflexible Children*. 5th ed. New York: Harper Paperbacks, 2014.

McCarthy, J., and J. Boyd. "Mental Health Services and Young People with Intellectual Disability: Is It Time to Do Better?" *Journal of Intellectual Disability Research* 46 (2002): 250–56.

McGuire, Dennis, and Brian Chicoine. *Mental Wellness in Adults with Down Syndrome: A Guide to Emotional and Behavioral Strengths and Challenges.* Bethesda, MD: Woodbine House, 2006.

Stein, D. S., K. Munir, A. Karweck, and E. J. Davidson. "Developmental Regression, Depression, and Psychosocial Stress in an Adolescent with Down Syndrome." *Journal of Developmental and Behavioral Pediatrics* 34, no. 3 (2013): 216–18.

Skotko, Brian, and Susan P. Levine. *Fasten Your Seatbelt: A Crash Course in Down Syndrome for Brothers and Sisters.* Bethesda, MD: Woodbine House, 2009.

Index

About the Author

D r. David S. Stein is a pediatric psychologist specializing in neuro-psychological testing, assessment of neurodevelopmental disorders, and behavioral and cognitive behavioral therapy. Dr. Stein is the founder of New England Neurodevelopment, LLC, in Concord, Massachusetts. He was on the faculty of Boston Children's Hospital and an instructor at Harvard Medical School from 2010 to 2016. Dr. Stein has spoken nationally and internationally regarding neurodevelopment and related disorders. He is the author of several scholarly articles, chapters, and this book.

Dr. Stein is a graduate of Tufts University and William James College. He completed his APA Internship in Child Psychology at Harvard Medical School/The Cambridge Hospital and his postdoctoral fellowship in Pediatric Psychology at Boston Children's Hospital and Harvard Medical School.